CW00572035

MACKAY HUGH BAILLIE SCOTT
An Architectural History

Design — Jonathon Jeffrey
© Amulree Publications
First published 1995

The publication of this book was made possible by financial assistance from the Manx Heritage Foundation.

Mackay Hugh Baillie Scott: An Architectural History (Paperback).
Printed by Spider Web Printing, 14–20 Sussex Way, London N7 6RS.

2

ISBN 0 952 1126 5 5

MACKAY HUGH BAILLIE SCOTT
An Architectural History

by Gregory John Slater

ACKNOWLEDGEMENTS

The author acknowledges with gratitude the assistance that he has received from the following:

For assisting with the preparation of the original thesis; Professor Charles H. A. MacCallum (formerly of Cardiff University, now Professor of Architecture, University of Glasgow and Head of School, The Mackintosh School of Architecture, Glasgow), all the staff of the Bute Library, The Welsh School of Architecture, Cardiff University and Debbie and Bill Toombs.

For their research assistance; Richard Tucker (Centre for Advanced Studies in Architecture, Bath University), Alan Franklin (Assistant Librarian, Manx National Heritage), Bill Calderhead (Secretary and Archivist, The Batheaston Society), Mr. S.R. Cosh (Association for the Study Preservation and Restoration of Mosaics), Mr. R.E. Field (ASPROM), The Rev. J.W.B. Perry (The Church of St. John the Baptist, Batheaston), The Rev. Duncan Whitworth (The Church of St. Matthew, Douglas), Barbara Holmes (Friends of the Royal Academy of Arts),

Brian Riddle, Martin Faragher, John Craster, Muriel Baird, Alan Kelly (Mannin Collections), Bernard Nurse (The Society of Antiquaries of London) and Mr. Coneybeare (Athol House, Batheaston).

For their assistance in the gathering of photographic contributions; Julian and Jenny Nutter (Bishop's Demesne), The Lord Bishop of Sodor and Man, Robert Elwall (RIBA Photographs Curator), Christopher Callow (Manx Diocesan Registrar), Mike Thompson (Eye of Man Photography),

Paula Lewis (Research Service Supervisor, Somerset Archives and Records Office), Nicola Gordon Duff (Sotheby's, London) and Ron Cooper.

But most particularly I would like to highlight the contributions of Mr. Peter Kelly (Victorian Society Caseworker for the Isle of Man), Patricia A. Tutt (Chartered Architect), Mrs. Marlene M. Hendy (Building Conservation Officer, The Isle of Man Government), Jonathon Jeffrey, Philip Eason and all associated with the Brow.

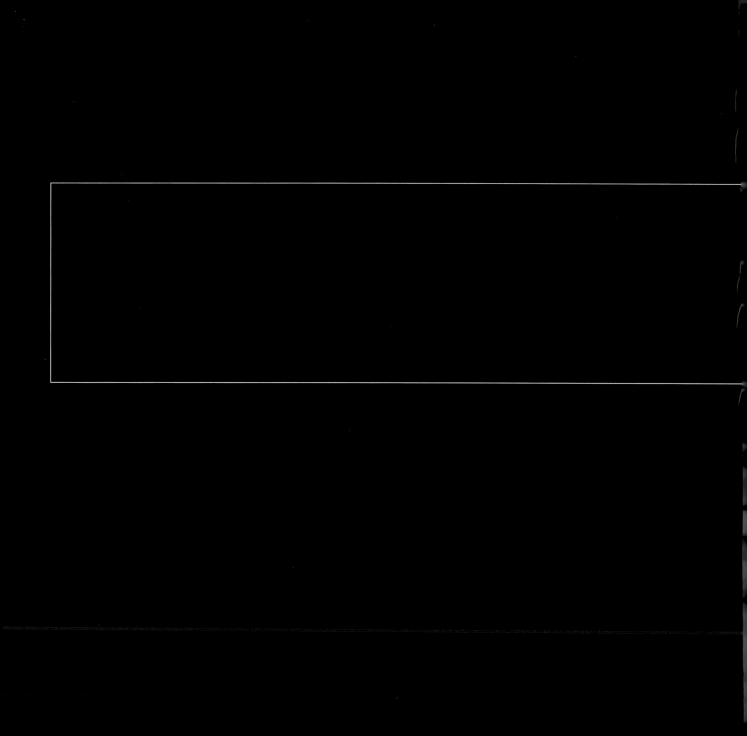

This book is dedicated to my parents, John and Helen Slater,
with great gratitude for their help and support throughout my training.

FOREWORD

Marlene M. Hendy

Building Conservation Officer
Isle of Man Government

It is indeed a pleasure for me to write the foreword to this important addition to the published information presently available on Mackay Hugh Baillie Scott.

The contribution of Baillie Scott to the architecture of the Arts and Crafts Movement should not be underestimated and it is heartening to detect signs that his true standing, in international terms, is at last being recognised.

Followers of Baillie Scott in the Isle of Man, in particular local architectural historian Peter Kelly, have over a considerable length of time been gathering further information on the architect's life and works during his Isle of Man period.

One of the most important aspects of this work by young author, Greg Slater, is that it presents some new information on Baillie Scott in a readable and accessible form, hitherto unavailable as such.

Since my appointment in May of this year, it has been a priority that the main group of Baillie Scott buildings in the Isle of Man should, at an early date, be entered in the Register of Protected Buildings: with this occurrence now imminent, it is appropriate that this volume will be available to provide a fitting insight into the works of this, one of the most talented architects to have visited our shores.

CONTENTS

BORN.ELDEST.BARON.HUGUENOT.FASHIONABLE.
SCHOOLED.UNIVERSITY.MANAGING.GRADUATED.
COUNTRYSIDE.ARTS.SKETCHING.ETHOS. ARCHITECT.
RADICAL.EMIGRATION.OPERAS.SAVOY.SISTERS.MILITARY.
REGIMENT.OFFICERS.FIERCE.INDIAN.CORONATION.ABBEY.
EMBROIDERED.ENGROSSED.COMICAL.BROTHER.
ARTICLED.PUPIL.SOANE.PEDIGREE.BATH.APPRENTICE-
SHIP.CHALLENGE.PERIOD.MEDIOCRE.VICTORIAN.WRITER.
DESECRATIONS.ANCERS.GEORGIAN.ERRONEOUSLY.
CRITICISM.ROMAN.DESPOILED.ARBITRATED.LEVIED.

A. **Mackay Hugh Baillie Scott, circa 1906.**
The Royal Institute of British Architects

1 — James D. Kornwolf, **M. H. Baillie Scott and the Arts and Crafts Movement: Pioneers of Modern Design**, (Baltimore and London: The Johns Hopkins Press, 1972), p.3. Note that one of the "not altogether dependable … biographical accounts" listed by Kornwolf in n.1 on the same page [A. Edgar Beresford, Architectural Reminiscences', **The Builder**, (10 August 1945), pp.104–109 (p.104)] states that Baillie Scott was "the eldest son in a family of nine children."

2 — IBID, p.3.

3 — IBID.

4 — Beresford, 'Architectural Reminiscences', p.104.

5 — IBID.

6 — IBID.

7 — IBID.

8 — Letter to Miss. E. J. Graves, dated 27 December 1915. Reproduced by kind permission of Manx National Heritage – Ref. MD 148-52-1.

Mackay Hugh Baillie Scott was born at Beards Hill, St. Peter's, near Ramsgate, Kent on October 23, 1865, "the eldest of fourteen children."[1] His father, also Mackay Hugh Baillie Scott, was a wealthy Scottish laird and owner of a valuable sheep farm in Australia. Although he was a Scottish baron, his title was not used by the family. Mrs Martha Baillie Scott, nee Waters, was from an English, "military family of Huguenot lineage."[2] They lived in the "fashionable district,"[3] St. Peter's, Broadstairs and then near Worthing, Sussex, where the young Baillie Scott was schooled with the intention that he would go on to Cambridge University. However, with a view to managing his father's Australian sheep farm, he was sent to the Royal Agricultural College, Cirencester in October 1883, to study for a degree in "scientific farming and estate management."[4] From here he graduated in December 1885, with honours in drawing and science and an inherent love of the countryside. A. E. Beresford, his later partner, also records that he won "the Society's Silver Medal."[5] From an early age, Baillie Scott had shown an interest in the arts, spending much of his time sketching landscapes and more "frequently, … old

Sussex farmhouses and churches"[6] in the South Downs. He was encouraged in this by his mother and probably, later, by drawing-masters at both Worthing and Cirencester. The love of nature and art he developed, was to be the foundation of his design ethos, and goes some way in explaining his decision to become an architect. Baillie Scott's own, rather unusual, reason for this radical change of plan, was that one evening during his visit to London early in 1886, initially made to purchase materials for his planned emigration, he went "to the Savoy Theatre, to which all London was then flocking to hear … the … comic operas of Gilbert and Sullivan and he was so enraptured that he decided forthwith that he would not be banished to the other side of the world where such delights were unobtainable, but would at all costs stay in England within reach of the Savoy."[7]

Little has been written of Baillie Scott's thirteen brothers and sisters. Two of his sisters are known to have married into the military: one to a Colonel Pritchard, who later "was in the midst of the action [during the First World War, losing]… most of his regiment and nearly all the officers"[8] in the fierce

9 — Letter to Miss. E. J. Graves, dated 27 December 1915. Reproduced by kind permission of Manx National Heritage – Ref. MD 148-52-1.

10 — Letter to Miss. E. J. Graves, dated July 1911. Reproduced by kind permission of Manx National Heritage – Ref. MD 148-50.

11 — IBID.

12 — Kornwolf, **M. H. Baillie Scott and the Arts and Crafts Movement**, p.545.

13 — IBID, p.5

14 — IBID.

15 — Peter Davey, **Architecture of the Arts and Crafts Movement**, (New York: Rizzoli, 1980), p.164.

16 — John Betjeman, 'M. H. Baillie Scott, FRIBA, An Appreciation by John Betjeman', **The Studio**, (July 1945), 17.

17 — Kornwolf, **M. H. Baillie Scott and the Arts and Crafts Movement**, p.6.

fighting; and the other, to a General who "had the military command in the colony."[9] The latter was "in command of the Indian Contingent"[10] at the Coronation of King George V in 1911 and got seats for Baillie Scott and his sister in the Abbey. In a letter to a Manx friend, Miss E. J. Graves (who embroidered designs for his furniture) Baillie Scott asked, whilst describing why he did not attend; "I wonder why you think I should be so engrossed with the Coronation – or perhaps you meant to be comical?… We discovered Court dress was required and so gave it up. Then we had some first rate seats in Constitution Hill but I by this time had got so utterly tired of our 'Sailor King' in the papers that I felt I would get away from it all so gave up the seats!"[11] A brother named Roderick has also been mentioned,[12] for whom Baillie Scott built 'Lower Meade', Templewood Lane, Stoke Poges, Buckinghamshire in 1910.

Between 1886 and 1889, Baillie Scott was articled to Major Charles E. Davis, City Architect of Bath. Davis had been the pupil of his father, Edward, who in turn had been a pupil of Sir John Soane. Such pedigree did not appear to favour Baillie Scott and it may not have been such a good idea to choose Bath or Davis for his apprenticeship: neither "offered the sort of challenge it was usual for architectural apprentices of that period to seek."[13] Davis had little, stylistically, to contribute to Baillie Scott, being "a rather mediocre High Victorian architect,"[14] whose 'Empire Hotel' was later described by the architectural writer Peter Davey as being, "until the desecrations of the last twenty years, … one of the few cancers on Bath's Georgian fabric."[15] According to Baillie Scott, himself, he learned only "to draw out the orders"[16] whilst with Davis and "apparently disliked the pompous 'Colonel' [as Davis was erroneously known] personally, as well as his architecture and the manner in which he conducted his practice."[17]

Baillie Scott was not alone in his criticism of Davis, who caused controversy during the construction of his new Queen's Bath and Pump Room, when the remains of Roman baths found on the site were despoiled. The core of the criticisms raised by the Society of Antiquaries (ultimately arbitrated by Alfred Waterhouse) were "archaeological and… levied less at the justifiable effort to provide modern bathing provisions at the

18 — Kornwolf, **M. H. Baillie Scott and the Arts and Crafts Movement**, p.6.

19 — **The Building News**, (December 18, 1866), p.870.

20 — Kornwolf, **M. H. Baillie Scott and the Arts and Crafts Movement**, p.6.

21 — IBID, p.7.

22 — IBID, n. 21.

23. — IBID, p.83.

24. — see panel

25. — Candidate's Statement for Fellowship by kind permission of the Royal Institute of British Architects.

26 — Allen Chandler, **Memoir of M. H. Baillie Scott**, (25 February 1967). Prepared for James Kornwolf.

27 — Letter to the author from Mr. S. R. Cosh, Hon. Secretary of the Association for the Study, Preservation and Restoration of Mosaics (ASPROM), 26 July 1995.

Athol House, Batheaston

The 1881 Census record identifies the occupants of Athol House as: Stephen Rawlings, head of the household and a mason and builder (age 45); his wife Emma (49); and their children, George (13 and described as a labourer with his father), Elisabeth (11), John (9) and Annie (2).

By the 1891 Census, 10 years later, Emma had only reached 53 years of age (a clerical error in one of the censuses) and all but the youngest child had moved out, although a grandson, Arthur Mules (4), had joined the family. The extra space was now being utilised, as it would have been by Baillie Scott during the intervening years, for lodgers. Those then registered were; Fritz Schultz (36, born in Prussia and described as a head brewer – presumably at the nearby Avonvale Brewery), his wife Marie (30) and Frederick Perret (34 and described as the manager of a corset factory).

Researched by Mr. Bill Calderhead, Secretary of the Batheaston Society (letter to the author dated 10 March 1995).

expense of some of the old remains, than at Davis' 'unprofessional' manner of restoration."[18] Davis' problems did not stop there. In 1886 a workman was killed when the newly built "east wall of the building, not being of sufficient strength to resist the thrust [of the arches, collapsed on him. The contractor was exonerated of all blame which seemed]… , in effect, to be a verdict against the City Architect."[19]

The "professional and public scorn that Davis [experienced at this time] … contributed to his eventual withdrawal from public office and may explain why Baillie Scott chose to remain aloof from all public commissions and, in fact, became hostile to public functionaries."[20] He must also have "pondered the fate which could befall the architect who either exceeded his abilities or did not practice moderation. [What is known about Baillie Scott's training would not suggest that he had a great knowledge of structures and in the light of his experiences with Davis], … it is perhaps not surprising that throughout his career he rarely attempted to design large or difficult structures."[21] He "appears to have built only one building of more than four stories and this was probably engineered by his [later] partner, A. Edgar Beresford."[22] Some more practical experience may have been gained when, "for at least one year of his stay"[23] in Bath, Baillie Scott lodged with a mason and builder, Stephen Rawlings,[24] who lived at Athol House, Batheaston. Many years later, in his candidate's statement for admission as a Fellow of the Royal Institute of British Architects, Baillie Scott also mentioned that he "went through the shops of various building trades."[25]

B. **The marble inlay paving at Kirk Braddan, Isle of Man, c. 1898–1899.**
Patricia A. Tutt.

28 — Identified by Mr. Peter Kelly, Victorian Society caseworker for the Isle of Man, in conversation with the author, 12 July 1995.

29 — John Betjeman, 'An Appreciation', p.17 and Kornwolf, **M. H. Baillie Scott and the Arts and Crafts Movement**, p.148, n.124 where Kornwolf mentioned that "no existing documentation connects Scott's name with these mosaics" and that there is "ambiguity on the matter."

30 — The Reverend Duncan Whitworth, Vicar of St. Matthew's Church, Douglas, in conversation with the author, 22 July 1995.

31 — Letter to the author from Mr. S. R. Cosh, Hon. Secretary, ASPROM, 26 July 1995.

32 — Letter to the author from Mr. R. E. Field, ASPROM, 13 August 1995.

33 — Kornwolf, **M. H. Baillie Scott and the Arts and Crafts Movement**, p.548.

34 — Letter to the author from Mr. R. E. Field, ASPROM, 13 August 1995.

Incidentally, he was employed, during the construction of Davis' Queen's Bath, on copying tessellated Roman pavements found on the site.[26] He was later able to utilise this experience gained in the use of old tile and mosaic materials when commissioned, towards the end of the nineteenth century, to design marble inlay paving (known as *opus sectile*[27]) for the chancel and sanctuary of John Loughborough Pearson's Kirk Braddan, Isle of Man[28] (originally completed in 1876). This work has been considered to be the product of a collaboration with Pearson at his St. Matthew's Church, Douglas, Isle of Man.[29] The paving that does exist at St. Matthew's, however, is quarry tiling as opposed to mosaic and is "nothing special."[30] Although this church was originally opened on 10 July 1901, the chancel was not completed and consecrated until St. Matthew's Day, 21 September 1908, by which time Baillie Scott had long since left the Island. The design of the paving, still to be seen at Kirk Braddan, matches that used in another of Baillie Scott's commissions, 'Blackwell' (a house at Bowness, Westmorland), built between 1898 and 1899. His additions to Kirk Braddan were probably undertaken around the same time. The design used by Baillie Scott is "certainly not directly related to any [Roman] mosaic from Bath, or from anywhere else in Britain."[31] It is thought that "the main inspiration… has come from the 'Cosmati' floors, [named after the Cosmati family who were working in the eleventh and twelfth centuries], that can be found in Italy, especially in Churches in Rome."[32] Although he later built a house in Italy,[33] it is unlikely that he would have travelled there at this early stage of his career and it is more probable that his source of reference, was one of "the many books of ornament which were published at that time."[34]

OCCASIONALLY.DESCENDENT.DANDY.CEREMONIES.
FASHIONABLE.MEDICINE.DEFECTS.INDIA.SAILING.
SEASICK.ANECDOTE.HUMOUR.INABILITY.TRAVELLED.
DELIGHTED.CONSEQUENCE.DUCAL.EMBARASSMENT.
CONVEYANCE.CAMBRIDGE.EXHAUSTING.FESTIVITIES.
OAR.CENSUS.SERVANTS.NURSE.RUSKIN.QUOTE.BRAIN.
INSPIRATION.COMPOSITION.GEOMETRY.AWARDS.
EXHIBITED.INDUSTRIAL.ACADEMY.VOICE.KNOX.OPINION.
ACCOMPLISHED.MUSEUM.DESCENDENTS.REPOUSS....
GULES.AVERSE.MANN.DOCTOR.DREADFUL.SURVIVE.

C. **The Baillie Scott's marriage register entry.**
Somerset Archives and Record Office.

D. **The half-timberwork of the nave roof (1865), the Church of St. John the Baptist, Batheaston. Note that this re-roofing was undertaken in the same year that Baillie Scott was born.** Philip Eason.

1 — Kornwolf, **M. H. Baillie Scott and the Arts and Crafts Movement**, p.83.

2 — David Crystal, editor, **The Cambridge Concise Encyclopaedia**, (Cambridge: Cambridge University Press, 1992), p.523

3 — John Betjeman, 'M. H. Baillie Scott', **The Journal of the Manx Museum**, Vol. VII, No. 84 (1968), pp. 77–80 (p.79)

During his time in Bath, Baillie Scott met and "occasionally entertained"[1] Miss Florence Kate Nash, a descendant of the Welsh dandy, Richard (Beau) Nash (1674–1762) who in 1705 had become the Master of Ceremonies of Bath, which place he "transformed into a leading fashionable centre."[2] Miss Nash's late father had practised medicine in India and she was born on board a sailing ship returning to England in 1862. They were married at Batheaston Parish Church on 16 February 1889, and then went for a holiday in the Isle of Man. The holiday became a 12 year stay, Baillie Scott later telling John Betjeman, when he was editor of the Architectural Review, " I went to the Isle of Man for a holiday. I was so seasick I couldn't face the journey back so I set up in practice there!"[3]

4 — John Betjeman, 'An Appreciation', p.17.

5 — Letter to Miss. E. J. Graves, dated July 1911. Reproduced by kind permission of Manx National Heritage – Ref. MD 148-50.

6 — 1891 census information reproduced by kind permission of Manx National Heritage.

7. — Kornwolf, **M.H. Baillie Scott and the Arts and Crafts Movement**, p.97.

This anecdote, however, serves to illustrate Baillie Scott's sense of humour rather than an inability to travel. He was, in fact, much travelled as a consequence of the many commissions he was to gain in Europe and delighted in telling of his arrival at the Ducal Palace at Darmstadt, where he later undertook some interior works, "of the great coach sent to meet him and of his embarrassment at seeing a second conveyance for his luggage, which consisted of one small bag."[4]

For the first four years of their stay in the Isle of Man, the Baillie Scotts lived at 35 Alexander Terrace, Douglas. On November 20, 1889, their first child, Enid Maud Mackay Baillie Scott was born, and on May 13, 1891, Mackay Hugh Baillie Scott III, affectionately known as Bi, was born. Both children eventually went up to Cambridge, as had been intended for their father who later recorded, in a letter to Miss. Graves, that Enid had been enjoying "the exhausting festivities of May Week, [attending] dances up till six in the morning… [and that he had gone] for a day to see the races where Bi – who is supposed to be a fine oar – was rowing."[5] It is recorded in the 1891 census[6] that the Baillie Scott's had two domestic servants living with them at

Alexander Terrace: a general servant, Margaret Abbot (aged 23) and a nurse for Enid and Bi called Dorothy Hull (aged 15). In 1893 the family moved to the 'Red House', Victoria Road, Douglas, designed by Baillie Scott himself. This he may have named after the house built for William Morris by Philip Webb in 1859, which would give an indication of his knowledge and appreciation of Webb's work and the associated writings of Morris and Ruskin, from which he would later quote on frequent occasions in his articles. On the other hand, as with later commissions such as 'The White House' and 'White Lodge', the colour of the materials used in the construction may be a more direct source of its title. The "obvious inspiration for the design was not Webb … [however] but Ernest George [1839–1922, and most particularly] his cottage at Harpenden, Hertfordshire [1887], where one may observe an almost identical composition and use of materials."[7]

To start with, Baillie Scott worked for Fred Saunderson, a surveyor and land agent whose office was located at 7 Athol Street, Douglas. In what was probably an attempt at filling some of the gaps left after his 'apprenticeship' in Bath, he attended classes in geometry and drawing at the Isle of

E. **The 'Red House',
Douglas, Isle of Man
(1892–1893).** The Author.

8 — Fine Art and Industrial Guild; Second (11–14 December 1889), Third (10–13 December 1890), Fourth (2–5 December 1891), Fifth (7–10 December 1892), Sixth (6–9 December 1893), Seventh (3–6 December 1894), Eighth (9–12 December 1895), Ninth (7–10 December 1896), Tenth (14–17 February 1898) and Eleventh (5–7 December 1899) Exhibition Catalogues. By kind permission of Manx National Heritage.

Man School of Art, also in Douglas. In May 1891, he gained the Art Class Teacher's Certificate, a national teaching standard set by the Department of Education and Science, South Kensington, having attained first or second place in all awards up to that date. Between December 1889 and December 1899 Baillie Scott exhibited paintings and other works at the Isle of Man Fine Art and Industrial Guild's second to eleventh exhibitions held at 'The Palace', Douglas[8] and from 1894 he began to regularly exhibit work in the Architectural Room of the Royal Academy of Arts, with as many

9 — Barbara Holmes, of the Friends of the Royal Academy of Arts, in conversation with the author – 22 July 1995.

10 — A. E. Beresford to John Betjeman, 10 October 1959, quoted from Kornwolf, **M. H. Baillie Scott and the Arts and Crafts Movement**, p.105, n.39.

11 — Kornwolf, **M.H. Baillie Scott and the Arts and Crafts Movement**, p.85.

12 — John Betjeman, M. H. Baillie Scott', p.79.

13 — Kornwolf, **M. H. Baillie Scott and the Arts and Crafts Movement**, p.104, n.36.

14 — Miss. Phyllis D. Wood, **Memoir of M. H. Baillie Scott**, (7 July 1955), p.8. Reproduced by kind permission of Manx National Heritage – Ref. MD 148 – 213.

15 — IBID.

as five entries in one year.[9] Beresford later told John Betjeman that "the R. A. … accepted everything he offered: he was a new voice."[10]

It was at the school of art that Baillie Scott met Archibald Knox, a member of the teaching staff at that time. Born in the Isle of Man in 1864, Knox was only one year Baillie Scott's senior, but a comparison of their paintings of the time by Baillie Scott's biographer, James Kornwolf,[11] showed Knox to be the more accomplished of the two, especially in water colour. It is these water colours which can be seen to be the first identified influence on Baillie Scott. Betjeman later wrote in the Journal of the Manx Museum that Baillie Scott's " daughter, Mrs Wallis, [as she had become by marriage],… remembers that [Knox]… worked on designs in [his]… office."[12] This does not necessarily mean that Knox worked directly for Baillie Scott as an assistant, but more likely that he collaborated with him on certain elements of his interior commissions. Descendants of two of Baillie Scott's clients have given accounts of his involvement. Mrs Helen Butler, daughter of Deemster Thomas Kneen (a Manx Justice) who commissioned him to

undertake interior works to 'Glencrutchery House', Douglas, told Kornwolf that "Knox… was responsible for executing the repoussé of the copper [fireplace] hoods [there and] … at 'Ivydene',"[13] Little Switzerland, Douglas. Miss. Phyllis D. Wood, niece of the aforementioned Miss. Graves and whose father Dr. Wood also had interior works undertaken by Baillie Scott, at 4 Albert Terrace, Douglas, wrote a journal of her memoirs of him in 1955. In it she wrote of interior works he undertook at 'Glen Falcon', also in Douglas. "The dining room and drawing room… had deep friezes down to the top of the doors, with falcons stencilled on the drawing room frieze and gulls with spread wings in the dining room. The friezes designed by Mr. Archibald Knox."[14] Although Baillie Scott liked to be in control of a complete commission, he was not averse to introducing elements of other designers' work, of which he approved, in this way. Miss Wood also remembered that "the curtains Mr. Scott chose for us were designed by Voysey – green with two birds on an island and one tree. Mr. Scott said it was like the Isle of Mann! He evidently considered we can have very few trees here."[15]

F. **Design for the Bates'
Bungalow, Douglas, Isle
of Man (1889–1890)**
'The Building News'
(18 July 1890).

16 — Beresford,
'Architectural
Reminiscences', p.104.

17 — John Betjeman, 'An
Appreciation', p.17.

18 — James D. Kornwolf, 'M.
H. Baillie Scott', in Adolf K.
Placzek, editor, **Macmillan
Encyclopaedia of
Architects Vol. I** (London:
The Free Press, 1982), p.129.

At about the same time as the move to the 'Red House', Baillie Scott left Saunderson and set up his own practice at 23 Athol Street, Douglas, which he soon moved into the 'Red House'. Baillie Scott gained many commissions whilst on the Isle of Man, although only a few were from Manx clients. His first did, however, come via Saunderson's office, from a doctor who had purchased some land through the firm. The brief was for an "ultra-hygienic house,"[16] the finished design of which Baillie Scott later described as "a dreadful affair."[17] The drawings do not survive, and it is thought that the house was never executed. The earliest surviving design, from 1889–1890, is a bungalow for a Mr. J. H. Bates, intended for Douglas, although never built. It derived heavily from American 'shingle-style' architects and was "quite similar to Frank Lloyd Wright's [1867–1959] earliest work."[18]

19 — John Fleming, Hugh Honour and Nikolaus Pevsner, **The Penguin Dictionary of Architecture**, (Middx; Penguin, 1987), p.109.

20 — Kornwolf, **M. H. Baillie Scott and the Arts and Crafts Movement**, p.97, n.29.

21 — M. H. Baillie Scott, **Houses and Gardens**, (London: George Newnes, 1906), p.78.

22 — Kornwolf, **M. H. Baillie Scott and the Arts and Crafts Movement**, p.152.

23 — Kornwolf, **M. H. Baillie Scott and the Arts and Crafts Movement**, p.89.

24 — M. H. Baillie Scott, 'An Ideal Suburban House', **The Studio** (January 1895), pp. 127-132 (p.127).

Baillie Scott's next published design, a proposed house, also intended for Douglas, owed little to the American influence to be seen in the 'Bates Bungalow,' but instead, drew from the burgeoning Arts and Crafts Movement, and the recent designs of Richard Norman Shaw (1831–1912), and as with the later 'Red House', Ernest George. It utilised Tudor half-timbering and had a Jacobean brick gable, "curved in the manner of the Netherlands,"[19] both features that would appear in much of his subsequent work. The use of these elements together with materials such as roughcast harling and red clay roof tiles, which were "hardly indigenous to the Island,"[20] was quite without precedent on the Isle of Man at this time. Baillie Scott thought that "in modern buildings, while we may well learn a lesson from the old work, in using local materials, it would be unreasonable to forego the opportunity modern transit affords of importing materials which are more suitable for our requirements."[21] His low commission rate on the Island may have been a result of the local tradition being broken in this way, although as his buildings started to become more fashionable, they began to be imitated, with Kornwolf describing a builder called

Cowle "who, like so many in his profession, succeeded in spreading Scott's style throughout the Isle profitably."[22]

As more commissions came in, Baillie Scott began to bring into his designs a flow of open space between rooms, that was to be seen in the designs of American architects, but that was "without precedent or parallel elsewhere."[23] The fact that he had to look to America to find precedent of a type which satisfied his design requirements, and that such planning was not characteristic (or to be found at all) in English design of the period, prompted him to start writing articles for the magazine 'The Studio'. The first such article was entitled 'An Ideal Suburban House' which, through the illustration of one of his designs, aimed to show how a few of the "most glaring defects"[24] of the average suburban house could be corrected. His buildings had already been illustrated in building magazines, but it was this article, and those that followed, which brought Baillie Scott to the attention of the public outside the Isle of Man, and led directly to his first commission from off the Island. 'Bexton Croft' was a slightly modified version of the design illustrated in the article

G. **Braddan Cemetary Office, Isle of Man, is thought to be Baillie Scott's earliest built work. The documentary evidence for this commission was located by Peter Kelly (Victorian Society caseworker for the Isle of Man) in the Braddan Vestry Minutes for 1892.** Patricia A. Tutt.

25 — Kornwolf, **M. H. Baillie Scott and the Arts and Crafts Movement**, p.145.

26 — IBID, p.5, n.12.

'An Ideal Suburban House', and was built in Knutsford, Cheshire (1894–1896). As well as frequently publishing his designs and articles, Baillie Scott later helped edit ' The Studio Yearbook of Decorative Art'.

Baillie Scott would have found it difficult to supervise the increasing number of commissions he received from England and in 1895 he formed a "working agreement, or partnership,"[25] with a close associate from his Bath days, Henry Seton Morris (born 1868). Morris, "perhaps a fellow pupil of Davis,"[26] opened an office in both names at 30 Great James Street, London in 1895 and was first involved with the building of 'Bexton Croft'. A number of works were published over the next two years, including

H. **'Bexton Croft',
Knutsford, Cheshire
(1894–1896), Baillie Scott's
'Ideal Suburban House'.**
'The Building News'
(26 June 1896).

27 — Peter Kelly, Victorian
Society caseworker for the
Isle of Man, in conversation
with the author (28 August
1995)

28 — Letter to Miss. E. J.
Graves, undated.
Reproduced by kind permis-
sion of Manx National
Heritage – Ref. MD 148-57-1.

a drawing, exhibited at the Royal Academy in the Spring of 1895, of an entrance to a house near Peel, Isle of Man. The client was the Manx author Hall Caine, about whose "long flowing red hair"[27] Baillie Scott later wrote one of his nonsense rhymes:

"I thought I saw a house on fire
 a blazing in the rain
 I looked again and saw it was
 a person called H[all] C[aine]
Oh! give to me those locks I said
 T'will benefit the brain."[28]

29 — Kornwolf, **M. H. Baillie Scott and the Arts and Crafts Movement**, p.145.

30 — IBID, n.118.

31 — IBID, p.147.

32 — IBID.

33 — IBID, p.148.

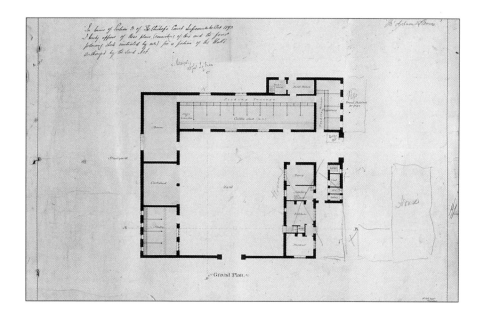

The entrance design, however, received an unfavourable review for its lack of domestic character and is thought to have had "more to do with Morris than with Scott."[29] The partnership does not seem to have been a fruitful one … [and, Kornwolf thought], because the two architects approached their art differently, differences of opinion on what should be published and whose name should be affixed to it caused the association to flounder"[30] in 1897. Another contributory factor may have been Baillie Scott's "association with Wilfred Bond"[31] who, in 1896, came from London to act as clerk of works on Pearson's St. Matthew's Church (another reason that has been used

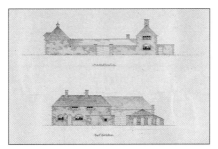

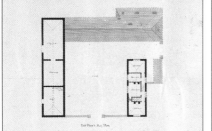

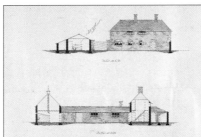

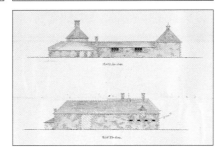

I. **The original drawings, recently discovered, for Bishop's Demesne, Bishopscourt, Isle of Man (1893–1894). This scheme for a model farm layout, researched by Peter Kelly, comprises a four bedroomed house adjoining a yard, around which are ranged; a barn, a four horse stable, a double cartshed, a twenty stall cowshed, a piggery, a root house, a boiler house, a granary and a thrashing mill. The farm was built by the Douglas based building firm of McAdam and Moore, following the passing of the Bishopscourt Improvements Act (1893) at Tynwald, the Manx Parliament. William McAdam also made the pulpit designed, by Baillie Scott, for St. Peter's Church, Onchan, Isle of Man. Baillie Scott was appointed architect, for Bishop's Demesne, on 23 May 1893, but it was not until 10 August 1893 that the contract, for this scheme and repairs to Bishopscourt Farm, was let. Given the nature of the site, a good distance off the road and high up in the hills, the completion date of 1 October was wholly inadequate. Additional work was agreed at a site meeting on 3 November and a special agreement was drawn up at the beginning of December, but by the beginning of January 1894, concern was being expressed over the delay to completion. The matter was still being resolved in August, but by this time, McAdam and Moore had gone into liquidation and on 24 July, McAdam had been declared a bankrupt. The farm, as built and surviving, varies from the drawings by virtue of the sensible decision to pull the house away from the smells of the farmyard, together with other minor alterations. It is not known whether the small ventilator above the stables was ever built, for no evidence of it remains. Much damage, in the form of unsympathetic modernisation, is currently being swept away by the farms new owners, in an effort to return the buildings to what Baillie Scott, who was paid £49.16s.0d. for the design and supervision, envisaged.** Sodor and Man Diocesan Registry.

to link Baillie Scott with the aforementioned mosaics at St. Matthew's). In Douglas, Bond "came into contact with Scott and his architecture and took a liking to both."[32] "Pearson died in 1896 and in 1898 Bond joined Baillie Scott as an assistant, [probably supervising works in England and] remaining with him until 1901."[33]

03

PERU.PAINTER.PALACE.COLLABORATION.GUILD.
INTERNEES.DETENTION.DENTIST.ATTRIBUTED.
CRAFTSMEN.CENSOR.PRINCESS.OFFSPRING.NEST.LOG.
ELEVATED.LIVING.FANTASTIC.ESCAPE.DRAWBRIDGE.
CABIN.TOWER.ELABORATELY.SPACE.MOTIF.PRINCIPAL.
SUNFLOWER.ORATORY.BEDCHAMBER.FINE.MANX.
EMBROIDERY.MENTIONED.DISFIGURED.SWALLOWED.
MAJESTIC.COMPLEX.SUCCESSFULLY.LOVER.
SPONSORED.EDITOR.PRIZE.JURY.SATISFYING.FULFILLED.
OBJECTIVE.ENERGETICALLY.SOLUTION.CONFRONTING.

1 — John Betjeman, 'An Appreciation', p.17.

2 — Kornwolf, **M. H. Baillie Scott and the Arts and Crafts Movement**, pp.546, 554 and 559.

The articles in 'The Studio' gained Baillie Scott commissions not only from England, but from Europe and occasionally further afield – John Betjeman listing "Germany, Italy, Poland, Russia, Austria, Rumania, America and Switzerland"[1] and Kornwolf further identifying buildings in Canada, Hong Kong and Peru![2] After the publication of another article in 'The Studio', October 1896, entitled 'An Artist's House', came a commission for a house in Brussels for the Belgian painter Willy Schlobach. This was followed, in 1897, by an important commission from the Grand Duke, Ernst-Ludwig of Hesse (Queen Victoria's grandson), to redecorate and furnish the dining-room and

K. **The desk built for Norman McArthur Douglas.** Sotheby's.

3 — Muriel Baird (niece of Douglas) in conversation with the author, 17 July 1995.

4 — Catalogue for Decorative Arts Sale, Sotheby's, Bond Street, 15 July 1983 – Lot no. 179.

5 — Kornwolf, **M. H. Baillie Scott and the Arts and Crafts Movement**, p.177.

6 — A. L. N. Russell, 'Houses by Baillie Scott and Beresford', **RIBA Journal** (17 June 1933), p.636.

7 — Tenth Fine Art and Industrial Guild Exhibition Catalogue (14-17 February 1898), entry no. 262. By kind permission of Manx National Heritage.

8 — Peter Kelly, Victorian Society caseworker for the Isle of Man, in conversation with the author (28 August 1995)

9 — Kornwolf, **M. H. Baillie Scott and the Arts and Crafts Movement**, p.101.

drawing-room of the Ducal Palace at Darmstadt. This was done in collaboration with C. R. Ashbee, whose Guild of Handicraft made the furniture, light fixtures and metal-work to Baillie Scott's designs, not the only time that his designs for furniture were executed by others. During the First World War, by which time Baillie Scott had left the Isle of Man, internees in the Manx Detention Camp for Civilian Prisoners of War at Knockaloe made a leaving present of a desk to their dentist, Norman McArthur Douglas (camp dentist between 13 November 1914 and 11 November 1918).[3] The design of the top, at least, has been attributed to Baillie Scott.[4] How it came into the possession of the internee craftsmen is not known. Knox was employed as a censor of the mail on the camp so it is possible that the design, probably produced at the School of Art, came from him.

In 1898 Baillie Scott was commissioned by the 23 year old Princess Marie of Rumania (a Hesse offspring), to decorate and furnish her Royal retreat. 'Le Nid', "the nest of the princess,"[5] was a treetop log cabin elevated to a height of over 25 feet, supported by living fir-trees within woodland at Sinaia, Rumania. It was a fantastic commission and was a place where Princess Marie could escape from the life of the palace, to the extent of being able to pull up a draw-bridge between the cabin and the adjacent stair-tower. It contained one of Baillie Scott's most elaborately designed interiors "in which each space had a different flower as the motif of its decoration:"[6] the sunflower for the principal space, the lily for the oratory alcove and the poppy for the bedchamber. At least one piece of furniture designed by Baillie Scott for 'Le Nid', a chair exhibited at the tenth Fine Art and Industrial Guild exhibition in Douglas,[7] was made by the Manx joiner and builder R. F. Douglas and had embroidery undertaken by Baillie Scott's wife, Florence. Douglas also constructed the previously mentioned 'Ivydene',[8] Baillie Scott's second largest Manx commission, next to the now horrendously disfigured 'MacAndrew House', 1892–1893, swallowed up as part of the Majestic Hotel complex. 'Ivydene' is considered by Kornwolf to be Baillie Scott's most successfully planned and executed house on the Isle of Man.[9]

L. **Groudle Glen Hotel, Isle of Man (opened August 1893), built for the same client as 'Ivydene', Richard Maltby Broadbent. This building has been identified as a Baillie Scott commission by Peter Kelly (despite the lack of any known documentary evidence), not least because of such typically Baillie Scott design features as the first floor windows 'hung from the eaves', see illustration P and the long, flat roofed dormers** **('possibly introduced to the Island by Baillie Scott'), see illustration Q, which it possesses. Also, it is unlikely that Broadbent would have employed two architects (one for the hotel and one for 'Ivydene') at the same time and Miss. Denver, the daughter of the licensees of the hotel during the inter-war period was told by Mr. R. G. Shannon, an accountant for a nearby estate company from the same period, that Baillie Scott undertook the commission.** Ron Cooper

10 — Quoted from Kornwolf, **M. H. Baillie Scott and the Arts and Crafts Movement**, p.216, and taken from 'Entscheidung des Wettbewerbes zur Erlangung von Entwurfen fur ein herrschaftliches Wohnhaus eines Kunstfreundes,' **Zeitschrift fur Innendekoration** (June-July 1901), pp. 109-113, (p.111).

11 — Kornwolf, **M. H. Baillie Scott and the arts and Crafts Movement**, p.216.

12 — Quoted from Kornwolf, **M. H. Baillie Scott and the Arts and Crafts Movement**, p.216, and taken from 'Entscheidung des Wettbewerbes zur Erlangung von Entwurfen fur ein herrschaftliches Wohnhaus eines Kunstfreundes', p.111.

13 — Quoted from Kornwolf, **M. H. Baillie Scott and the Arts and Crafts Movement**, p.219, and taken from 'Entscheidung des Wettbewerbes zur Erlangung von Entwurfen fur ein herrschaftliches Wohnhaus eines Kunstfreundes', p.111.

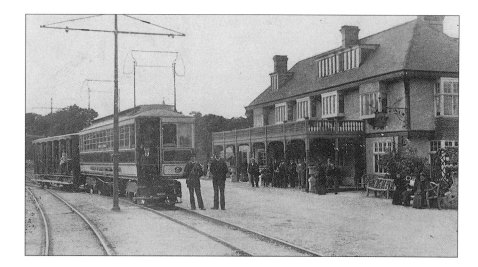

In 1901, Baillie Scott entered the 'Haus eines Kunstfreundes' or 'House for an art lover' competition, sponsored by Alexander Koch, editor of the 'Zeitschrift fur Innendekoration' magazine, from Darmstadt. The first prize was not awarded, as the jury thought that although the competition had produced "satisfying results,"[10] none of the 36 entries had "entirely fulfilled the objective of the competition,"[11] which was "to contribute energetically to the solution of important questions confronting modern architecture."[12] Baillie Scott's design, entitled Dulce Domum' was, however, awarded the highest prize of 1800 marks (originally intended as second prize). The jury were most impressed with his "masterfully handled interiors,"[13] and would have awarded first prize, were it not for the historicist elevations.

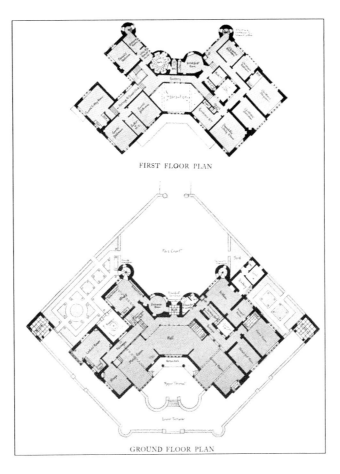

FIRST FLOOR PLAN

GROUND FLOOR PLAN

M. **Plans for the 'House for an Art Lover' competition entry (1901).** M. H. Baillie Scott, 'Houses and Gardens', (London: George Newnes, 1906).

The first prize of 8000 marks was split between more than sixteen of the submitted designs, three of which were given third prize (Leopold Bauer, Oscar Marmorek and Paul Zeroch). C. R. Mackintosh had also entered the competition, and although his design entitled 'Der Vogel' had been disqualified for not containing the required number of interior perspectives, it must have pleased the judges, as it was awarded a purchase prize of 600 marks.

04

RELOCATED.PRESSURE.RESENTED.INDISCRIMINATE.
UNINSPIRED.FLATTERED.REALISATIONS.JUSTICE.
CONCEPTIONS.SCRUPULOUS.CONSIGNED.LIBERTY.
UNSYMPATHETIC.ADAPTATIONS.REPUTABLE.
APPROPRIATE.CONTEMPORARIES.CARICATURES.
DISCREDIT.PROFESS.COLLABORATOR.COPIES.THRIVED.
DESTINATION.PYGHTLE.SURMISED.MANUFACTURE.
ARTISTIC.CONSEQUENT.ADVANCED.SLATER.SWIRLING.
APPROVED.ABANDONED.PASSION.NONDESCRIPT.
RESTORATIONS.AMUSEMENT.FRUSTRATINGLY.RAPPORT.

1 — Kornwolf, **M. H. Baillie Scott and the Arts and Crafts Movement**, p.157.

2 — IBID, p.155.

3 — Baillie Scott, **Houses and Gardens**, p.3.

4 — Wood, **Memoir of M. H. Baillie Scott**, p.6.

5 — Martin Faragher, Alfred and Archibald', **Victorian Society Journal**, no.20 (Spring 1987), pp.7–10 (p.7).

At the time the 'Haus eines Kunstfreundes' competition was being judged in Darmstadt (May 16 and 17, 1901), Baillie Scott sold the 'Red House' and by the middle of that same year, the family had relocated to Bedford. The move resulted partly from the rising pressure of commissions from England and abroad, and perhaps also because he "strongly resented the imitation of his houses… and their indiscriminate replication"[1] in multiple housing schemes, as demonstrated by Fred Saunderson's proposed 'Cliftonville' estate in Onchan, which was "little more than a totally uninspired multiplication seventy times over of… houses by Baillie Scott."[2] In 1905 he wrote: "since January 1895, when I first illustrated in the Studio a scheme for a house, I have been flattered by many realisations of my plans for houses in various parts of the world. While some have had the justice to realise that an artist should be given the opportunity of developing his own conceptions, others less scrupulous have consigned the matter to other hands and the plans have suffered much from unsympathetic treatment in this way. So much depends on the careful working out of the details to meet each particular case, so

much in the choice of materials and in adaptations to local conditions, that a plan realised in this way must necessarily differ widely from the original conception; and in as much as it is not the reputable architect who is willing to appropriate the plans of his contemporaries, these houses have been for the most part merely caricatures, which have done much to bring undeserved discredit on the principles they profess to follow."[3] This also accounts for Baillie Scott falling out with his former collaborator, R. F. Douglas. When Miss. Wood's Aunt asked "point blank why he did not like a builder, R. F. D., he answered 'because he copies my designs'."[4]

Bedford may have been chosen as the Baillie Scotts destination, either because the children were to be sent to school there, or more likely so that Baillie Scott could be closer to the 'Pyghtle' Works of John P. White, for whom he had been designing furniture since 1898. This furniture was sold at White's showroom at 134 New Bond Street and through Liberty's (to which it has been "surmised"[5] that Baillie Scott introduced Knox). By 1901 it was possible to publish a catalogue of 120 pieces for manufacture, by

6 — John Betjeman, Mackay Hugh Baillie Scott', p.79.

7 — Hermann Muthesius, **Das Englische Haus** (Berlin: Wasmuth, 1904-1905).

8 — Kornwolf, **M. H. Baillie Scott and the Arts and Crafts Movement**, p.244.

9 — IBID.

10 — Allen Chandler, **Memoir of M. H. Baillie Scott**, (25 February 1967). Prepared for Kornwolf.

11 — Kornwolf, **M. H. Baillie Scott and the Arts and Crafts Movement**, p.342, n.157.

12 — IBID.

White, to Baillie Scott's designs. Baillie Scott obviously thrived in the artistic company he would have met on his consequent visits to London and described to John Betjeman how "advanced architects… like himself always ate in Slater's tea shops. This was a matter of principle because the tea shops with their huge, circular entrances of bent glass and their swirling staircases within, were in an art nouveau style of which… he approved."[6]

Although Baillie Scott did prepare a design for a new house (known only from an illustration of the plan, to be seen in Hermann Muthesius' volume 'Das Englische Haus'[7]), this was abandoned and instead he pursued a growing passion for "old work,"[8] by linking and restoring two "rather nondescript"[9] early nineteenth century cottages. Located on the outskirts of Bedford, 'Fenlake Manor' was the first of many such restorations, for his own use or amusement. From an office at 4 Windsor Place, St. Cuthbert Street, Bedford (until 1903) and then from 'Fenlake Manor' he continued his practice but, frustratingly for Baillie Scott, despite his efforts at building a rapport with the townspeople of Bedford, he never gained a commission there, and only a few from the surrounding villages of Bedfordshire.

In 1904 Baillie Scott became involved with the Garden City Movement, the brainchild of Ebenezer Howard, as it was being developed by the architects Barry Parker and Raymond Unwin at nearby Letchworth (the first garden city, started in 1903) and Hampstead. Kornwolf thought Charles Paget Wade, "a brilliant black and white illustrator"[10] who "drew many of the maps and plans for England's garden cities and suburbs,"[11] "may… have been Scott's link with the movement, for in the twenties, [according to Kornwolf, Wade] … commissioned Scott to carry out extensive repairs and additions to his house, 'Snowshill Manor', near Broadway,"[12] Worcestershire. It is not thought, however, that Baillie Scott did in fact do any work to this house, but its gardens were laid out to his designs. The commission came about after Baillie Scott met Wade during the development of Hampstead Garden Suburb rather than as suggested by Kornwolf. It is the only surviving independent garden layout designed by Baillie Scott, which also incorporates structures designed by Wade, and is now in the care of the National Trust.

'Elmwood Cottages', a pair of semi-detatched houses, were the first of four houses Baillie Scott built at Letchworth,

13 — Kornwolf, **M. H. Baillie Scott and the Arts and Crafts Movement**, p.305.

14 — IBID, P.312.

15 — Duncan Simpson, 'History of Taste, 3: Beautiful Tudor', **Architectural Review**, Vol. 162 (July 1977), pp. 30–36 (p.33).

N. **Waterlow Court, Hampstead Garden Suburb (1909).**
'The British Architect,' (9 July 1909).

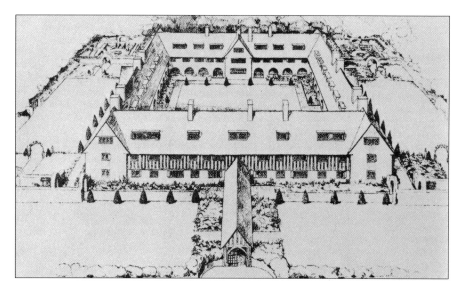

designed in 1904 and subsequently approved by Parker and Unwin the following year. They were built at 7–7a Norton Way North as part of the 'Cheap Cottage Exhibition' that same year, at a cost of £420. More interesting were Baillie Scott's contributions to Hampstead Garden Suburb (begun in 1905), though sadly only two of the five or more schemes prepared were built. The first, designed for plot 400, Meadway, and unbuilt, is seen as "the finest of all his designs for the garden city,"[13] and marks the expansion of his planning vocabulary into multiple housing schemes. A variation of this scheme was built, albeit "on a more modest scale,"[14] as 'Waterlow Court', on Hampstead Way. Not only important for being the largest and only completed example of Baillie Scott's multiple housing schemes, Waterlow Court was "socially avant-garde,"[15] advancing the theme of communal living and being a

16 — Brigid Grafton Green, **Hampstead Garden Suburb 1907–1977 : A History**, (Hampstead Garden Suburb Residents' Association and author, 1977), p.16.

17 — Kornwolf, **M. H. Baillie Scott and the Arts and Crafts Movement**, p.312.

18 — IBID, p.543.

19 — Baillie Scott, **Houses and Gardens**, p.83.

20 — IBID, p.6.

21 — IBID, pp.86, 87.

22 — IBID, p.86.

23 — IBID, p.36.

24 — Letter to Miss. E. J. Graves, undated but known to be referring to the 1906 volume of **Houses and Gardens** as written from 'Fenlake Manor.' Reproduced by kind permission of Manx National Heritage – Ref. MD 148-55.

25 — Kornwolf, **M. H. Baillie Scott and the Arts and Crafts Movement**, p.xxix.

26 — IBID, p.xxx.

specialised scheme intended for "that rare [in 1909] animal, the working lady."[16] Containing 50 flats of three or four rooms each, the occupants could cater for themselves if so desired, but the provision of common dining and living rooms on the ground floor obviated the "need for the single dinner and lonely evening that can follow it."[17] In arranging the flats around an inner, grassed courtyard, a secure and protective environment was created. Baillie Scott also built a house or houses at Hellerau Garden City in Germany but the "exact extent of [the] commission [and whether this scheme was undertaken are] unknown."[18]

In 1906, Baillie Scott published a volume, titled 'Houses and Gardens', in which he aimed "to show what is possible for the average householder… in the planning of… [a] house and its surrounding garden."[19] Pitched against "the majority of small houses… designed and built by men who have no knowledge or skill in planning and whose notions and habits of thought are entirely commercial,"[20] he described his creation, 'The Artistic House', "rationally designed on economical lines"[21] and which "is artistic in proportion to the amount and quality of the skill and thought displayed in its design and not in proportion to the amount of decoration it possesses."[22] Every conceivable space and feature of the house received its own chapter, right down to "accommodation for family pets,"[23] in which his ideas for what are now known as 'cat flaps' were considered! Differing house types were also covered, with chapters on terraced houses, cottages, semi-detached houses, holiday homes, flats and co-operative housing, all elaborated on by the inclusion of illustrations and descriptions of a number of his commissions to date. The diversity of the buildings illustrated and the varied and complex problems solved therein, coupled with their extensive distribution world-wide, served to illustrate the breadth of Baillie Scott's design ability and showed how widely acknowledged he was by this time, although primarily abroad. He told Miss Graves: "I hope my book may be published in the Autumn. It is difficult to make great progress with a job when nobody cares whether it is finished or not, except perhaps on the continent and [in] America"[24] where, incidentally, Kornwolf thought that Baillie Scott's "especially pure and mature"[25] designs of this period (1902 – 1907) had an "influence… deeper and more crucial in some ways than Voysey's or Mackintosh's."[26]

05

RESPONSIBILITY.TECHNICAL.EXPANDING.EFFICIENCY.
INSTINCTS.ROMANTIC.INTENSIVE.DOMESTIC.
PREFERENCE.RESTORING.SCOFFER.ORTHODOXY.HERALD.
PORTENT.METICULOUS.WANDERING.CHIPPIES.RECTORY.
IMPRESSIVE.ACTIVE.LIMITATIONS.EMULATED.GLOOM.
ABERRATION.HANGING.WITTY.REJOINDER.ROOKERY.
SHOVE.DISASTER.DESTROYED.FEATS.HUMOUR.FAKE.
INDULGING.UNSATISFACTORY.DEPOSITED.TRAIN.
DURATION.BARRAGE.FATE.NAVAL.SPECULATIVE.DESPAIR.
DESPERATE.ANCHORAGE.FLOURISHED.MODEST.

1 — Kornwolf, **M. H. Baillie Scott and the Arts and Crafts Movement**, p.397.

2 — IBID.

3 — Beresford, Architectural Reminiscences', p.105.

4 — IBID, p.105.

5 — IBID.

6 — Kornwolf, **M. H. Baillie Scott and the Arts and Crafts Movement**, p.432, n.43.

In 1905 Baillie Scott employed an assistant, A. E. Beresford, who took over "responsibility for the financial and technical aspects of the expanding practice,"[1] leaving Baillie Scott free to concentrate on the process of design. "Beresford's efficiency and professional instincts,"[2] resulted in a much more organised and stable practice and contributed greatly to its continuing success. Born and schooled in Macclesfield, Cheshire, Beresford had temporarily entered the office of a "friendly country builder… [fully intending to move on to a position with a local bank. However, he found that he] preferred the exciting and romantic adventure of building… and within very few weeks was 'bound apprentice' to the trade for six years, during which… [he] laid bricks, cut stone on the 'banker' and spent nearly two years at the joiner's bench."[3] He became more and more " keenly interested in the design of buildings and the drawing of plans [and decided he] wanted to be an architect rather than a builder… There followed a few years' intensive study, both in class and with a private coach and… [after] assisting various Manchester architects – mostly in domestic and church work,"[4] applied for the advertised

position of chief assistant to Baillie Scott. Soon after becoming his assistant, Beresford asked Baillie Scott why he had chosen him in preference to others more qualified, who had also applied. Baillie Scott replied that "it was largely due to… [his] reference to restoring some fine old Cheshire farmhouses, from which he saw that… [Beresford] loved old work as much as he did'. [This puzzled Beresford who described how],… in those days, Scott was generally believed to be a rebel, a scoffer at orthodoxy [and] the herald of a new style which owed little or nothing to the traditions of old work."[5] As will be seen, this was an early portent of the future.

The high quality of craftsmanship to be seen in Baillie Scott's houses of the period, is attributable to the "meticulous supervision"[6] of another of his assistants, Jack Pocock, son of the architect Maurice Pocock. He was used by Baillie Scott as a "wandering clerk of the works, to show the brickies how to do their job. He used to kick over their wall (when it was too mechanically laid), grab the trowel and build a bit himself…. [He] also showed the chippies how to use an adze on the oak timberwork and

7 — Chandler, **Memoir of M. H. Baillie Scott**'.

8 — Kornwolf, **M. H. Baillie Scott and the Arts and Crafts Movement**, p.249, n.15.

9 — M. H. Baillie Scott, 'The Cheap Cottage', **The Studio** (March 1914), pp.133-139.

10 — Kornwolf, **M. H. Baillie Scott and the Arts and Crafts Movement**, p.398, n.7.

11 — Kornwolf, **M. H. Baillie Scott and the Arts and Crafts Movement**, p.432, n.43.

12 — IBID.

13 — Beresford, 'Architectural Reminiscences', p.108.

14 — IBID.

15 — Letter to Miss. E. J. Graves, dated March 1911. Reproduced by kind permission of Manx National Heritage – Ref. MD 148-51.

beams [which another assistant, (Allan Chandler, thought Baillie Scott]… would have liked… to have been cut by a pair of top-and-bottom sawyers in the woods, but the day of the power-driven buzz-saw had arrived!"[7] Chandler worked in Baillie Scott's offices in Bedford (1910–1914) and later London (1920–1924). Whilst in the London Office. he undertook the design of 'The Rectory', Derby Road, Haslemere, Surrey (1922).

A. Percival Starkey was yet another assistant at this time (1907–1914), who undertook the design, "which is not impressive,"[8] for a Bedfordshire cottage illustrated in Baillie Scott's article 'The Cheap Cottage'.[9] "After the War, Starkey established his own practice at Dunsmor, South Hill Avenue, Harrow, Middlesex, where he was active until the late thirties."[10]

It is interesting to note that, aware of his own limitations, Baillie Scott was keen that all his pupils, in some contrast to himself, "learned by doing"[11] and he sent "Chandler, Pocock, Beresford, Starkey and others into White's shop at Bedford to learn the crafts."[12] The training Baillie Scott offered

may have been too successful for when, in 1907, Starkey and Beresford "emulated him in submitting drawings to the Royal Academy,"[13] their works were exhibited and his not. A few days after learning this, Baillie Scott "related, in an assumed gloom, the latest aberration of the 'hanging committee'… [to his friend, White' who] had, as usual, a witty and apt rejoinder. 'Opposite my house', he said, 'there is a rookery which I often sit and watch, and at this time of year you can see an exactly similar thing happening. As soon as the young birds get big enough, they just shove the old birds out of the nest!' "[14]

The practice prospered until, in March 1911, disaster struck. The house and office at Fenlake, along with most of the records and drawings from this period, were destroyed by fire. Baillie Scott wrote: "in the remnants of the house, my assistants and I are achieving feats of memory in reproducing lost plans. What we shall do next, I don't know."[15] Despite this air of great loss, Baillie Scott was still able to show his humour, writing to Miss Graves shortly afterwards, "did you ever have a fire?… We have just been indulging in that

16 — Letter to Miss. E. J. Graves, dated March 1911. Reproduced by kind permission of Manx National Heritage – Ref. MD 148-51.

17 — IBID.

18 — Kornwolf, **M. H. Baillie Scott and the Arts and Crafts Movement**, p.443.

19 — Chandler, **Memoir of M. H. Baillie Scott**.

20 — Letter to Miss. E. J. Graves, dated 27 December 1915. Reproduced by kind permission of Manx National Heritage – Ref. MD 148-52-1.

21 — Kornwolf, **M. H. Baillie Scott and the Arts and Crafts Movement**, p.444.

22 — IBID.

23 — Beresford, 'Architectural Reminiscences', p.108.

24 — Kornwolf, **M. H. Baillie Scott and the Arts and Crafts Movement**, p.444.

25 — Letter to Miss. E. J. Graves, dated 27 December 1915. Reproduced by kind permission of Manx National Heritage – Ref. MD 148-52-1.

26 — IBID.

experience!"[16] The office was moved to Beresford's house at St. John's Street, Bedford, where it remained until 1914. To start with, the Baillie Scotts stayed with a friend, "Colonel Dubois, in a fine old house called 'The Rams'."[17] They then took rooms in a boarding house, 'Riversley', Rothesay Road, Bedford. "These lodgings proved quite unsatisfactory"[18] and they soon moved to 'The Lodge' at Elstow, where they stayed until the Autumn of 1912. It was here that Mrs. Baillie Scott was on the receiving end of her husband's sense of humour. As recalled by Chandler: "walking to 'Elstow Lodge' for lunch one day from the St. John's Street office, we stopped at the bank to collect the family silver which was deposited there after the fire. It was the best part of a mile walk, the box was heavy and the day was hot. So he suggested hiding the box behind a hedge and telling Mrs. Scott that it had been stolen! And we did. And she believed us. She, poor lady, had no sense of humour!"[19]

Beresford stayed on in Bedford, but for the next few years Baillie Scott moved his family from place to place. First they went to London, "to try life in a Kensington flat,"[20] but "life in London did not agree with the Baillie Scotts"[21] and in 1913 they settled in Haslemere, Surrey, where Chandler's family lived. Business was "carried out by train"[22] until the outbreak of the first World War, when the practice was finished for the duration. Beresford, in his own words, was " ill-adapted for military service [and] worked awhile with a… famous surveyor in the city [and] then was asked to become a temporary servant of the Admiralty… [He] enrolled as the first draughtsman of a new section just formed to organise the production of… 'kite balloons',… used… for observation purposes"[23] and later for barrage. In the meantime, the Baillie Scotts had moved again, this time to Farnham in Kent, where Baillie Scott's daughter Enid had some friends. "In less than a year, they shuttled from one furnished house to another,"[24] one of which was "a little parson's house."[25] "Then fate began giving [the family]… various hard knocks."[26] Enid's fiance, Gordon Gray, was killed in naval action off Cape Horn, (he went down on the Good Hope') and her brother was married "against the family's wishes,"[27] "on the strength of getting a very good government appointment in East Africa … . Enid, being rather dull, thought it would be a good idea to try Bedford again for a bit"[28] and the

27 — Kornwolf, **M. H. Baillie Scott and the Arts and Crafts Movement**, p.444.

28 — Letter to Miss. E. J. Graves, dated 27 December 1915. Reproduced by kind permission of Manx National Heritage – Ref. MD 148-52-1

29 — IBID.

30 — Kornwolf, **M. H. Baillie Scott and the Arts and Crafts Movement**, p.445.

31. — There is some confusion regarding the name of this property. Betjeman, 'Mackay Hugh Baillie Scott', p.78 gives the name as 'Ockhams', whereas Kornwolf, who was in correspondence with its then owner, Mr. C. MacTaggart (who had purchased directly from Baillie Scott), amended this to 'Oakhams' – Kornwolf, **M.H. Baillie Scott and the Arts and Crafts Movement**, p.453 ff.

32 — IBID, p.443.

33 — IBID, p.411.

34 — M. H. Baillie Scott, 'Letter to the editor', **The British Architect**, (9 December 1910), p.400.

family moved to another parson's house at 13 St. Michael's Road. Incidentally, Enid later married D. L. Wallis, who had worked in Baillie Scott's office for a time and was the son of a speculative builder for whom Baillie Scott designed a number of houses in the late twenties and early thirties.

The Baillie Scotts stayed in Bedford until 1916, when they were able to move to 'The White House', Great Chart, near Ashford in Kent. Baillie Scott had purchased this fifteenth century Kentish farmhouse because of his "desperate desire for some sort of anchorage."[29] It's restoration and remodelling had taken nearly two years, "but no sooner had it been completed than he sold it and in 1918 the Scotts landed in London again, after spending a short period in Bath,"[30] at Bromley House in Russell Street.

With the end of the war in 1919, Baillie Scott and Beresford restored their practice, this time as partners. They opened an office at 8 Grays Inn, Holborn and the business quickly flourished. Baillie Scott undertook the restoration of, first, a seventeenth century house at 8 Quarry Street, Guildford, Surrey and then, between 1920 and 1921,

yet another house he had purchased for the family. 'Oakhams'[31] was a modest fifteenth century farmhouse off Marsh Green Road, Edenbridge, Kent which, like 'The White House' at Great Chart, typified the beliefs to which the once innovative Baillie Scott had descended during these chaotic times, that "no architect, least of all himself, could hope to compete nor want to compete with the 'beauties of old buildings'."[32] Baillie Scott's designs from this period reflected this belief, as his design language degenerated evermore into a language of pastiche, in which he aimed to "fake the antique."[33] This he did, designing overtly period buildings from as early as 1908 ('Burton Court', Longburton, Dorset). In 1910 he wrote, arguing against building by-laws, "the best service you can render to the artist in building is to give him freedom – the freedom which in the past has resulted in that beauty of old buildings which is the despair of the modern architect to equal."[34] Here began a "relentless campaign against officialdom, which culminated in an address before the Royal Institute of British Architects in 1929,"[35] together with an article 'Are Building Bye-laws Destructive of Rural Beauty?'[36] in the RIBA Journal. Baillie Scott,

O. **Burton Court,
Longburton, Dorset
(1908–1909).** 'The British
Architect', (7 May 1909).

Elevation from SOUTH - *Garden Front*

35 — Kornwolf, **M. H. Baillie
Scott and the Arts and
Crafts Movement**, p.403.

36 — M. H. Baillie Scott,
'Are Building Bye-Laws
Destructive of Rural Beauty?',
**The Journal of the Royal
Institute of British
Architects**, (January 1930),
pp.143-154.

37 — Kornwolf, **M. H. Baillie
Scott and the Arts and
Crafts Movement**, p.405.

38 — Chandler, **Memoir of
M. H. Baillie Scott**.

39 — M. H. Baillie Scott,
'Letter to the editor', **The
Builder**, (4 August 1944),
p.86.

40 — Tim Benton and Sandra
Millikin, **Art Nouveau 1890-
1902** (Milton Keynes: The
Open University Press,
1975), p.24.

however, "learned to circumvent the local by-laws by various means."[37] Chandler, who had previously been a council surveyor in Guildford, recalled visiting a new house built for a retired canon. The plans showed that the windows in a major room were less than one-tenth the area of the floor space and he realised that "the windows must be enlarged before any conscientious surveyor would pass the house. But on measuring the floor area of the room, I found that now they need not be and I knew what the architect had done. He had simply made the floor area smaller by temporarily boarding in the walls and papering them. As soon as I had gone, the reverend occupier would remove the boarding."[38]

Baillie Scott was not an advocate of the "so-called modern houses… [with their] enormous windows which afford the rooms little protection from external conditions. There is usually an enormous window on the staircase where little light is required. The garage doors are the most prominent feature suggesting that the most important thing in the house is the means of escape from it, while the inevitable flat roof combined with large glass areas still further fail to protect the house from the weather, with which the radiators are engaged in a losing battle."[39] The function and consequent size of every window in Baillie Scott's houses were carefully considered to attain the desired effect. He particularly "liked to use

41 — Davey, **Architecture of the Arts and Crafts Movement**, p.169.

42 — IBID.

43 — IBID.

44 — IBID.

45 — Kornwolf, **M. H. Baillie Scott and the Arts and Crafts Movement**, p.432.

46 — Beresford, 'Architectural Reminiscences', p.106.

47 — M. H. Baillie Scott and A. E. Beresford, **Houses and Gardens** (London: Architecture Illustrated, 1933).

48 — Kornwolf, 'M. H. Baillie Scott', p.130.

49 — IBID.

50 — Henry-Russell Hitchcock, **Architecture: Nineteenth and Twentieth Centuries**, (Baltimore: 1958), p.277.

51 — Kornwolf, **M. H. Baillie Scott and the Arts and Crafts Movement**, p.481.

windows as part of a seating niche, allowing you to look out if you wanted to, but not big enough to allow people to see in."[40]

It is unlikely that Baillie Scott needed to continue his practice for financial reasons, as "he owned, amongst other property, the Kensington Palace Hotel,"[41] but he continued to attract clients. The new fashion "was for Neo-Georgian discipline,"[42] and although Baillie Scott stood out against it for as long as he could, in 1913 he had had to fall in with his clients' taste and design his first Neo-Georgian house. It was the "antithesis of everything Scott had stood for up to that time,"[43] with his "plan contorted to allow the windows to be arranged in regular rows."[44] But despite his desire to make his buildings "look old at all costs"[45] and compromising his beliefs, this latter period was his most productive, with at least 130 buildings being built between 1919 and 1939. Beresford wrote: "we did not consider we were fully occupied unless we had at least twenty-five to thirty houses going up simultaneously, and these were not repetitions or even variants of the same plan; each was individually designed and fully detailed, room by room, however small or inexpensive."[46]

On 20 June 1927, Baillie Scott was elected a Fellow of the RIBA by Council and he served on the Arts Committee of the Institute from 1928 to 1930. His practice was moved to the nearby Bedford Row in 1930 and in 1933, he and Beresford (who Baillie Scott and others had nominated for fellowship in 1932) published a second volume of 'Houses and Gardens'.[47] The first volume had shown Baillie Scott to be a pioneering spirit in the formative years of the Arts and Crafts movement, but this second volume "defending what… [that] movement, once radical ethically… , had devolved into,"[48] facetiously pitted this ' traditional' architecture against "Modernist, flat-roofed anti-vernacular architecture,"[49] which the pioneers of the new machine age were putting forward in the 1920s and 1930s. The writer Henry-Russell Hitchcock thought it "hard to believe that the projects published… [were] by the same man."[50]

By 1935, Baillie Scott was becoming "weary…of his practice"[51] and came to the office less often, preferring to paint "flowers, rural scenes and fairy tale environments."[52] With the outbreak of war and the death of his wife, in 1939, Baillie Scott finally gave up his active practice and after "a few

52 — Kornwolf, **M. H. Baillie Scott and the Arts and Crafts Movement**, p.481.

53 — IBID, p.482.

54 — IBID

55 — IBID

56 — IBID, p.482.

57 — IBID, p.485.

months, "[53] Beresford wound up the office of Messrs. Baillie Scott and Beresford. But it was 1941 when Baillie Scott's career was truly terminated, as bombs destroyed the Bedford Row office, taking with it those drawings which had survived the uncannily similar disaster at Fenlake in 1911, along with everything that had been executed since that date.

"Beresford hoped to revive the practice at the end of the War but never did so."[54] Instead he relocated to New Quay, Cornwall, and "for a while was employed by the Claypool Tile Company designing prefabricated houses and bathrooms. A rather sad end."[55]

Baillie Scott sold 'Oakhams' in 1942 and under the care of a nurse, Ellen Brook, spent the next couple of years "in various nursing homes and cottages in Devon and Cornwall,"[56] keeping up with his painting. In August 1944 he wrote to 'The Builder' in favour of the emergency prefabricated dwellings that had recently been illustrated therein. Later that same year he and his nurse left Devanshire for 'Ripley House', Brighton.

On February 10, 1945, Mackay Hugh Baillie Scott died at the Elm Grove Hospital, Brighton. The epitaph "on the simple cubic stele that marks his grave in the country churchyard at Edenbridge"[57] reads 'Nature he loved and next to nature, Art'.

06

ORIGINS.HISTORICAL.PASSIONS.FLEMISH.CHARMING.
INDIVIDUAL.FANTASY.DESIRE.BLOSSOMING.
SHAPELESSLY.RECAPTURE.SPIRIT.INSPIRED.FONDNESS.
DOMINATED.COMPLEXITY.MATURED.PURER.MASSING.
EXPANSES.DISCARDED.SEVERE.FUNCTIONAL.CRISP.
DELICATE.SIMPLICITY.FENESTRATION.MINIATURES.
HORIZONTALITY.SHEER.APPRECIATED.PANORAMA.
REVOLUTIONISED.IMPRESSION.ABSORBED.SETTING.
COMPETITORS.CONTEMPORARY.REMINISCENT.STYLING.
TAPESTRY.ELABORATE.COLLABORATIONS.PERUSAL.

1 — Nicholas Taylor, 'Interior: Baillie Scott's Waldbuhl', **Architectural Review**, 138 (December 1965), pp. 456-458 (p.456).

2 — A. Edgar Beresford(F), 'Obituary: M. H. Baillie Scott (Ret. F.)', **RIBA Journal**, 52 (March 1945), p.143.

3 — IBID.

4 — Kornwolf, **M. H. Baillie Scott and the Arts and Crafts Movement**, p.108.

5 — IBID, p.109.

6 — IBID, p.184.

7 — IBID, p.132.

8 — IBID, p.134.

9 — IBID.

10 — IBID.

11 — IBID.

The exteriors of Baillie Scott's buildings had their origins in historical forms, his particular passions being for half-timbering, Flemish gables and pepperpot towers. He created charming and individual buildings rooted in fantasy, with irregular forms resulting from his desire to make "his houses sprout entirely from the inside, blossoming freely and often shapelessly without."[1] He aimed not to reproduce the "characteristic externals of a past style,"[2] but attempted to recapture "the essential spirit which inspired mediaeval craftsmen."[3] The use of half-timbering especially expressed his "fondness for materials and exposed structure,"[4] a theme which he "carried through to the inside"[5] of his buildings, to the extent that it dominated many of his principal rooms, as in the great hall at 'Blackwell'. Entirely half-timbered, this 28 feet by 46 feet, two-storey hall is "unmatched in scale and complexity"[6] by any other in Baillie Scott's designs.

Influenced by C. F. A. Voysey, Baillie Scott's use of half-timbering reduced as his style matured. With a desire to create purer forms, period detail was gradually stripped away, as he began to rely more on the massing of his buildings. On the road frontage of 'Myrtle Bank' and 'Holly Bank' (1895–1896), a pair of semi-detached houses on Victoria Road, Douglas, the half-timbering was used only to frame "large expanses of roughcast."[7] And on the garden facade, as described by James Kornwolf; "barge-boards, half-timber work, leaded-windows and gables… [were] discarded for an extremely plain, severe, but well-proportioned expanse of brick, roughcast and tile. The severe and purely functional character of the facade confirms Scott's debt to Voysey, but the crisp, flush surfaces, the light, delicate proportions and the simplicity of the fenestration are entirely Scott's."[8]

At 'Leafield' and 'Braeside', another pair of semi-detatched houses on King Edward Road, Onchan, Isle of Man (1896–1897), half-timber work was left only in a "series of very low dormer gables."[9] Along with the two matching porches, like "miniatures of the houses,"[10] the dormer windows served to relieve the horizontality of the otherwise roughcast rendered building that was, as Baillie Scott told Betjeman, the "favourite of all his works."[11]

12 — Kornwolf, **M. H. Baillie Scott and the Arts and Crafts Movement**, p.136.

13 — IBID.

14 — IBID.

15 — IBID.

16 — IBID, p.140.

17 — IBID.

18 — The Isle of Man Weekly Times (26 November 1898). Reproduced by kind permission of Manx National Heritage.

19 — IBID.

20 — IBID.

21 — Baillie Scott, **Houses and Gardens**, p.3.

22 — Kornwolf, **M. H. Baillie Scott and the Arts and Crafts Movement**, p.265.

By 1897, with the building of four terraced houses on Falcon Cliff, Douglas, half-timber work was completely absent. Their "sheer, unadorned wall surfaces"[12] of roughcast, derived from the garden facade of 'Myrtle Bank' and 'Holly Bank', are best appreciated when seen "against the cluttered panorama of late nineteenth century Douglas."[13] They "revolutionised the taste of the Isle"[14] and it is thought by Kornwolf, that had they been published, they may have made "a greater impression than Voysey's contemporary design for terrace houses at Brackley."[15]

At times, Baillie Scott's exteriors showed the considerable influence he absorbed from his contemporaries. His "most Voysey-like building,"[16] considered by Kornwolf to be "a tribute to Voysey's distinctive contribution to the architecture of the decade,"[17] is the Sunday School and Village Hall at Onchan (1897–1898). "His plans were selected by the committee from amongst a number of competitors"[18] and the completed building described in a contemporary report as "one of the finest buildings of its kind in the Isle of Man."[19] The hall is almost entirely rendered with white roughcast and has buttresses very reminiscent of Voysey's 'Perrycroft', on the

Malvern Hills, Herefordshire (1893). A wrought iron railing, a stained-glass window above the stage, both very 'Art Nouveau' in their styling, together with "the Voysey tapestry of the curtain and platform"[20] provided the only decoration, although an elaborate fresco was planned for the interior, but never executed.

Influence also came from Edwin Lutyens' houses, together with his garden planning collaborations with Gertrude Jekyll. In his introduction to 'Houses and Gardens', Baillie Scott wrote: "to those who wish to study the subject [of gardens], I would recommend a careful perusal of Miss. Jekyll's books which may be taken as an infallible guide."[21] The massing and fenestration of the garden facades of Baillie Scott's 'Heather Cottage', Sunningdale, Berkshire (1904), are very similar to Lutyens' 'Deanery Gardens', at nearby Sonning (1899–1901), being dominated by a central, projecting, glazed bay containing the hall. On planning terms, however, "there is less relation between the two houses: Lutyens' arrangement of the main rooms may well have been inspired by Scott's in other houses."[22]

P. **'Holly Bank', Little Switzerland, Douglas, Isle of Man (1895–1896).** Patricia A. Tutt

Q. **'Braeside', King Edward Road, Onchan, Isle of Man (1896–1897).** Patricia A. Tutt

R. **Terraced housing, Falcon Cliff, Douglas, Isle of Man (1897).** Patricia A. Tutt

S. **Onchan Village Hall and Sunday School, Isle of Man (1897–1898).** Patricia A. Tutt

T. **This design, for a House and Garden in Switzerland (1903–1904), demonstrates the influence of Edwin Lutyens and Gertrude Jekyll merged with Baillie Scott's own principles, to create a scheme very much his own.**
M. H. Baillie Scott, 'Houses and Gardens', (London: George Newnes, 1906).

23 — Kornwolf, **M. H. Baillie Scott and the Arts and Crafts Movement**, p.255.

24 — IBID, p.258.

25 — IBID, p.259.

26 — IBID.

27 — IBID, p.258.

28 — IBID, P.272.

29 — IBID, p.310.

30 — IBID, p.259.

Further influence from 'Deanery Gardens' had been developed in Baillie Scott's design for a cottage, 'Springcot' (1903), his earliest surviving design "complete with a garden setting."[23] Here, the double entrance doors opened into a "gallery-corridor,"[24] perhaps derived from the "covered passageways for vehicles, to stable courts in medieval inns or manor houses,"[25] (although a "more immediate source"[26] was 'Deanery Gardens'). It had a glazed wall along one side to the central hall and at its opposite end, further double doors opened into a 'garden room', Baillie Scott's precursor to the conservatory, outlined in a chapter of his first volume of 'Houses and Gardens'. "The mall-corridor [as Kornwolf termed it, achieved]... a new kind of flow of indoor-outdoor space directly through the center of the house."[27] This continued out into the garden, through the use of a vista (discovered in Lutyens' and Jekyll's garden books), across a court and through a long, linear pergola to a water garden at the extent of the site. Baillie Scott often used courtyards, terraces and formal gardens, in this way, as "an extension of indoor space,"[28] that gave his plans a "sense of 'organic' integration"[29] and at 'Springcot', where the house "was reduced to a mere incident in the overall plan, [created] a plan primarily concerned with outdoor space as a living area."[30]

Baillie Scott continued to refine the exteriors of his buildings and his pursuit of a pure form was best achieved at the 'White House', Helensburgh, Scotland (1899–1900), built near to where Mackintosh built his famous 'Hill House', two years later. Windows were set flush to the white, roughcast wall surface, and eaves

U. **'Springcot' (1903).**
M. H. Baillie Scott, 'Houses
and Gardens', (London:
George Newnes, 1906).

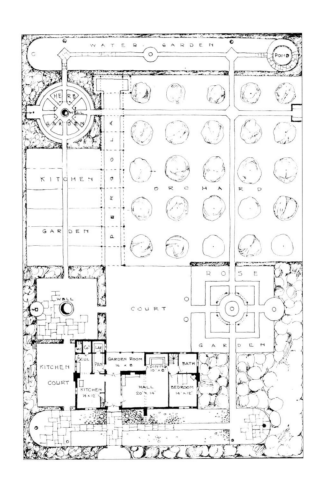

V. **'The White House',
Helensburgh, Scotland
(1899–1900).** M. H. Baillie
Scott, 'Houses and Gardens,'
(London: George Newnes,
1906).

31 — Kornwolf, **M. H. Baillie
Scott and the Arts and
Crafts Movement**, p.189.

32 — IBID, p.202.

33 — IBID, P.203.

eliminated "in order to preserve the exterior as one crisp, unpunctured and homogeneous whole"[31] and "to prevent any play of light and dark that would obscure the pure white form."[32] Whilst mentioning Mackintosh, it is interesting to note that, although evident in the Scottish Baronial Castles that were to influence the Scottish architect Robert Stoddart Lorimer (1864–1929), the "turreted, cylindrical stair-tower"[33] Mackintosh used at 'Hill House',

had been seen by him more recently, when competing against Baillie Scott's 'Dulce Domum' design for the 'Haus eines Kunstfreundes' competition. What prompted Baillie Scott to utilise this device is less clear. Also evident in his police station at Castletown, Isle of Man, designed just before 'Dulce Domum' in 1900, the former's low round tower is a contextual response to the fourteenth century, flanking barbican

W. **Castletown Police
Station, Isle of Man (1900).**
Patricia A. Tutt.

34 — G. F. Clucas,
Peel Castle. Isle of Man,
(Douglas: Brown and Sons,
1924), p.18.

35 — M. H. Baillie Scott,
A Note on Peel Castle',
The Builder's Journal,
(2 September 1908), p.156.

towers of 'Castle Rushen' opposite.
The low towers of the castle are, however,
castellated and do not explain the source
of the conical roof. It is possible that the
inspiration came from the Celtic round (or
peel) tower at Peel Castle, Peel, Isle of Man,
dating from the turn of the eleventh century
and of a type to be found in Ireland. Although
its roof would no longer have been evident
in Baillie Scott's time, an engraving from
1656[34] clearly shows that it was turreted.
It is quite possible that Baillie Scott, who
wrote an article titled 'A Note on Peel
Castle'[35] in 1908, was aware of this fact.

07

DESIGN.FURNISHED.MERGED.CONSISTENTLY.
COLORATION.CONSIDERABLE.STATIONARY.RELATIONSHIP.
REALISED.AUTONOMOUS.ART.UNDERSCORING.
STRIPPED.EXEMPLIFYING.RICHLY.PLEASURE.PEDESTAL.
REVEALED.DISTRACTING.MAXIMUM.SADNESS.CHIEFLY.
IRONY.RESPONSIBLE.SYMPATHETIC.REALISE.QUOTED.
INDUSTRIALISTS.ORNATELY.SURVIVES.ACHIEVE.RECORD.
ENLIGHTENED.STRIVING.MENTIONED.CUSTOM.
REPRESENTATIVE.PERIODICAL.RECOGNISING.INDIVIDUAL.
COMMERCIAL.MERELY.WORTHY.FASHION.ARCHIVIST.

1 — Muthesius,
Das Englische Haus, p.51.

2 — IBID.

3 — IBID.

4 — IBID.

5 — Baillie Scott,
Houses and Gardens, pp.3,4.

6 — Muthesius,
Das Englische Haus, p.51.

7 — Kornwolf, **M. H. Baillie Scott and the Arts and Crafts Movement**, p.117.

8 — Benton and Millikin, **Art Nouveau 1890–1920**, p.29.

9 — David Wainwright, **The Pianomakers** (London: Hutchinson, 1975), p.117.

10 — Kornwolf, **M. H. Baillie Scott and the Arts and Crafts Movement**, p.127.

To Baillie Scott, his houses were not just plans and elevations and from the very start of a design, he considered how the rooms inside would look when fully furnished and occupied. He merged architect and interior designer, so that his houses became an "organic whole to be designed consistently inside and out,"[1] with each room considered an individual creation that sprang from the overall idea. Muthesius saw this as a considerable "advance on the London movement,"[2] which had "remained stationary at the point to which Morris had taken it,"[3] as "in fact (had) England as a whole."[4] In 'Houses and Gardens' Baillie Scott wrote: "it has always seemed to me impossible to consider the matter of furniture and decoration apart from housebuilding, with which they are so intimately related and the architect who attempts to achieve a satisfactory interior, must necessarily to some extent control these important factors."[5]

The design and position of every piece of furniture was carefully considered within the rooms created by Baillie Scott, as was the positioning of doors and windows, creating a relationship that "realised the new idea of the interior as an autonomous work of art."[6] He preferred his furniture to be built-in, underscoring "his principle that interior space should be mainly open space."[7] He often stripped the detail from the outside of his pieces, further simplifying the space that they occupied, and then richly decorated the inside, so that the colours remained "in one's mind, even when the doors were closed, as a sort of private, secret pleasure."[8] In 1896, with this in mind, Baillie Scott designed his first piano. From outside it appeared to be "a plain closed cupboard on a pedestal, [but] when the doors with their 'wrought-iron' mediaeval hinges were folded sideways and back, the keyboard, music stand and candle-holders were revealed."[9] This prevented the piano from striking "a distracting note"[10] and became a recognised design, named the 'Manxman', in recognition of Baillie Scott.

Baillie Scott was not always able to undertake the complete commission that he would have liked, however, and it was with a hint of sadness that, in looking back over his work for the first publication of 'Houses and Gardens', he remarked; "one is chiefly struck by the strange irony of fate which has made one's employment consist of building

X. **Another German interior commission, the music room for Carl Reiss, Mannheim (1906).**
M. H. Baillie Scott, 'Houses and Gardens', (London: George Newnes, 1906).

11 — Baillie Scott, **Houses and Gardens**, p.235.

12 — IBID

13 — IBID, pp.235,236.

14 — Kornwolf, **M. H. Baillie Scott and the Arts and Crafts Movement**, p.129. n.99.

15 — Leslie Hoskins, Archivist, Arthur Sanderson & Sons Ltd. in conversation with the author, 22 August 1995.

houses for other people to furnish, or furnishing houses which other people have built. In no single case in the houses illustrated by photographs am I responsible for the furniture and the sympathetic reader will perhaps realise this."[11] He was, however, later to receive the complete commission he had been looking for, when asked to design a house, together with its interiors, furniture and garden, for the Swiss industrialist, Theodore Bühler. 'Landhaus Waldbühl', Uzwil, Switzerland (1907–1911), a particularly fine and ornately decorated scheme which still survives in the ownership of the Bühler family, demonstrates what Baillie Scott could achieve, given the support of a wealthy and enlightened client – Bühler had already read 'Houses and Gardens' and thus knew exactly what Baillie Scott was striving for.

At Darmstadt, as has been mentioned, Baillie Scott's task was "to decorate and furnish only."[12] This led to further German interior commissions including some for "exhibition rooms, designed for firms in Berlin and Dresden. [He explained;] it appears to be a growing custom with the principal furniture firms in Germany to invite representative architects to contribute to such periodical exhibitions and in these it has been Mr. Mackintosh and myself who have represented the British section. In thus recognising the claims of the individual artist in this field of design, these German firms seem to set an example which might well be followed in this country where, so far, furniture is still considered a commercial product, merely, and its design as hardly worthy of serious study as an art."[13] In a similar fashion, Baillie Scott later built a house (number 27) at the 1932 Home Arts Exhibition, Olympia, London.

As well as furniture, Baillie Scott, like Knox, also produced designs for wallpaper. Some were produced for the Deutsche Werkstätten at Dresden and the Wiener Werkstätte – two Arts and Crafts colonies in Germany. It was thought that some were designed for Sanderson's, as it has been written that he built two houses for the family.[14] However, Sanderson's archivist, Leslie Hoskins, thinks that this is "very unlikely"[15] as their well kept design log shows no record of this and the two buildings quoted ('Pilgrims', near Pilgrims Way, Chilham, Kent – 1912 to 1921 – and 'Two

Y. **Light fitting in the dining room of 'Glencrutchery House', Douglas (1897–1898). This building's interiors were described by Kornwolf, in the light of the destruction of those at Glen Falcon, Darmstadt, Le Nid and Mannheim, as especially valuable, being the earliest surviving and worthy examples of Baillie Scott's interior design. Despite this, the dining room interior was removed for auction as recently as 1992! The light** fittings remain on the Isle of Man as part of a private collection, but the current whereabouts of the room's panelling and ornate fireplace, somewhere in Germany, is unknown. The fireplace of the drawing room, removed some years previously, now resides in the Wolfsonian Foundation, Miami Beach, Florida. Mannin Collections.

16 — Kornwolf, **M. H. Baillie Scott and the Arts and Crafts Movement**, p.321.

17 — The Isle of Man Times (5 December 1891)

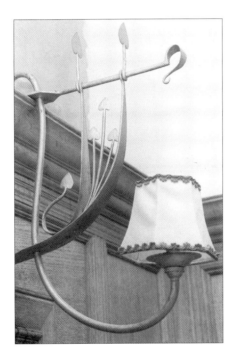

Ways', Old Mill Lane, Bray-on-Thames, Berkshire – 1921–1922) are not known addresses of the wallpaper branch of the Sanderson family at this time. Baillie Scott also produced designs for "many tapestries, rooms and household objects"[16] for manufacture at the Deutsche Werkstätten and as early as 1891, Bridgewood and Sons manufactured his designs for pottery.[17]

08

1 — Kornwolf, **M. H. Baillie Scott and the Arts and Crafts Movement**, p.91.

2 — IBID.

3 — IBID.

4 — Reyner Banham, 'Proof of Baillie Scott' **Architectural Review**, 153 (January 1973), p.79.

5 — Walter L. Creece, **The Search for Environment: The Garden City Before and After**, (New Haven and London: Yale University Press, 1966), p.297.

6 — Baillie Scott, **Houses and Gardens**, p.14.

7 — Taylor, 'Baillie Scott's Waldbuhl', p.456.

8 — Muthesius, **Das Englische Haus**, p.49.

9 — IBID, p.130.

10 — William Morris, A Dream of John Ball', first published in **Commonweal** (1886-1887) but quoted from M. H. Baillie Scott, **Houses and Gardens**, p.17.

It was Baillie Scott's experiments in planning that were his greatest achievements. It was described by James Kornwolf as "the most advanced planning of its kind in Europe"[1] "until the publication of Wright's work in 1911"[2] and important enough to elevate him "to a position of importance in the history of modern architecture."[3] Reyner Banham thought it "subtle enough to make Lutyens look coarse, [and] ingenious enough to make Voysey look crude."[4]

Baillie Scott's vital characteristic was the "rebellion"[5] against the room as an enclosed box which, like Wright, he so disliked. He wrote: "in making the plan for a house it will be necessary to banish from one's mind the conception of its interior as a mere group of isolated compartments and to think of it rather as a central room surrounded by subordinated ones, some of which may in many cases form either recesses in the central apartment or communicate with it either by folding or sliding doors."[6] The opening up of his plans stemmed from his "rediscovery of the hall as the central, living-dining-sitting…space,"[7] an often two-storey space, from which opened the other principal rooms of the

house. Muthesius likened this to a Roman villa in which the rooms "opened off the atrium,"[8] and saw "the spacious kitchen-living-room"[9] of old English farmhouses as the source of Baillie Scott's inspiration for its re-introduction. Baillie Scott hinted at this himself when, in his chapter titled 'The Hall' in his first volume of 'Houses and Gardens', he quoted from Morris' 'A Dream of John Ball': "the room we came into was indeed the house, for there was nothing but it on the ground floor, but a stair in the corner went up to the chamber or loft above."[10]

In his own 'Red House', Baillie Scott bounded two adjacent sides of the central hall with the drawing room and dining room. These were separated from the hall by hinged, wooden panels which could, on occasion, "be opened and flattened to the walls,"[11] avoiding the "usual humdrum box-like division of the rooms."[12] Baillie Scott explained; "by this means, the inconvenience which arises from the inevitable smallness of rooms in a house where economy is to be studied is obviated, and in a small house on festive occasions, a large amount of space can be obtained."[13] This arrangement was the "most important

11 — Kornwolf, **M. H. Baillie Scott and the Arts and Crafts Movement**, p.100.

12 — Muthesius, **Das Englische Haus**, p.49.

13 — Baillie Scott, 'An Ideal Suburban House', pp. 127-128.

14 — Kornwolf, **M. H. Baillie Scott and the Arts and Crafts Movement**, p.100.

15 — IBID.

16 — IBID, p.97.

17 — IBID.

18 — IBID, pp. 97,100.

19 — Baillie Scott, 'An Ideal Suburban House', p.128.

20 — Kornwolf, **M. H. Baillie Scott and the Arts and Crafts Movement**, p.108.

21 — Hermann Muthesius, 'M. H. Baillie Scott,' **Dekorative Kunst**, 5 (1900), pp.5-7 and 40-48 (p.6).

22 — Kornwolf, **M. H. Baillie Scott and the Arts and Crafts Movement**, p.108.

23 — IBID.

innovation at the 'Red House',"[14] and was "surely one of the most significant architectural advances in the period,"[15] that Baillie Scott continued to perfect in the plans of his subsequent houses.

Baillie Scott aimed to remove the function of circulation from the hall so that, when closed off, it could become a private family room in which they could remain undisturbed. To this end, at the 'Red House' he removed the main circulatory element, the stair, and created "a separate compartment, or stair-corridor, adjacent to, but distinct from, the hall."[16] It was more a space than a corridor, integrated with the stair, such that it became a more "positive element in the design."[17] It served "as a subtle, visually complex transition to changes in level – up to the bedrooms and down to the kitchen and servant areas."[18] This characteristic differentiation between living and service areas was introduced at 'Oakleigh', Douglas (1892–1893) and is expressed on the facades of his early houses, through the use of different materials for ground and first floors.

At 'Bexton Croft', circulation was entirely removed from the hall, by providing a gallery linking the porch to the drawing room, and the servants' domain of kitchen, pantry and scullery to the dining room and stairs. This enabled the hall to become the living core, where the family could retire "without being disturbed by servants passing through it, or without being obliged to hastily decamp on arrival of an unwelcome visitor."[19] Baillie Scott, with his 'Ideal Suburban House', had transformed the hall into the ultimate living space, with its importance as the core of his houses emphasised by its central position, its two-storey height, the removal of circulatory functions (stair and corridor) and its relationship with the drawing and dining rooms. "Communication was encouraged between the three living areas"[20] by the "broad openings"[21] and "above them by an open music gallery between the principal bedrooms."[22] Described by James Kornwolf as "transparent passages,"[23] they implied "an approach to planning by area rather than by room… [that was] symptomatic of Scott's debt to American planning, although his is more sophisticated. To find all these features in single examples of American or English

24 — Kornwolf, **M. H. Baillie Scott and the Arts and Crafts Movement**, p.108.

25 — IBID, p.97, n.31.

26 — IBID.

27 — Baillie Scott, **Houses and Gardens**, p.54.

Z. **'Bexton Croft', Knutsford, Cheshire (1894–1896). Ground and first floor plans.**
M. H. Baillie Scott, 'Houses and Gardens', (London: George Newnes, 1906).

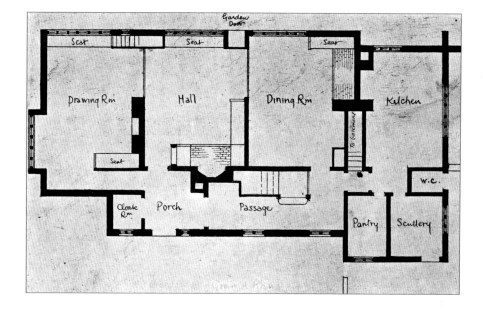

domestic architecture at this time is difficult… . In this respect, Baillie Scott must be compared not with Voysey but with Wright"[24], although unlike Baillie Scott who "increasingly focused his planning around the hall,"[25] Wright's plans were hinged around a central hearth or fireplace – Baillie Scott's "core was a space [and] Wright's a mass."[26] This is not to say that the fireplace did not have its own importance to Baillie Scott. He wrote that "in the house, the fire is practically a substitute for the sun and it bears the same relationship as the sun does to the landscape."[27]

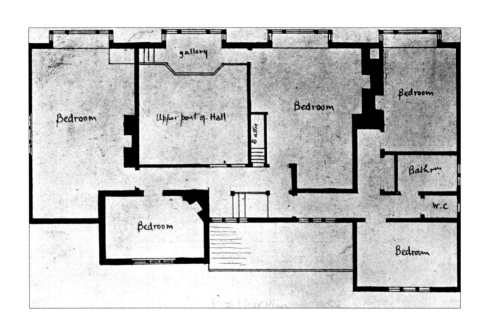

gallery

Bedroom

Upper part of Hall

Bedroom

Bedroom

Bathrm

w.c

Bedroom

Bedroom

1 — Banham, 'Proof of Baillie Scott', p.79.

2 — Russell, 'Houses by Baillie Scott and Beresford', p.636.

3 — Kornwolf, **M. H. Baillie Scott and the Arts and Crafts Movement**, p.321.

4 — IBID, p.391.

5 — IBID pp.391,392.

6 — IBID, p.118.

It is true that, at first sight, many of Baillie Scott's buildings may appear to be rather "unremarkable."[1] In 1933, A. L. N. Russell wrote of Baillie Scott and Beresford; "it may be doubted whether there are any of their contemporaries who have built so much all over England and done so little violence to its amenities."[2] However, a closer inspection reveals Baillie Scott to be one of the pioneering innovators of his time, who had a greater influence on others than he is often given credit for. On July 18, 1890, his 'Bates Bungalow' design was published in 'Building News' and from this date onwards, his advances in open planning were widely published. Kornwolf went so far as to state that "no English architect … was better known or appreciated in Germany before World War 1 … [and this was primarily due to the fact that he] had published more than a score of illustrated articles in 'The Studio', the harbinger of taste throughout Europe and America"[3] (published in the USA as 'International Studio').

James Kornwolf wrote of Frank Lloyd Wright's "indebtedness"[4] to the Arts and Crafts movement and "the likelihood of specific stylistic influences upon his architecture and theory, from Voysey and Baillie Scott in particular."[5] "Wright's basic dynamism may prevent one from accepting the importance of influence from such an architect as obviously undazzling as Baillie Scott, but it may at least be admitted that both architects are without peer in this decade for their radical integration of interior form and Baillie Scott was first to achieve this goal."[6] "It should [also] be remembered that of the nine points which … [Wright] listed at Princeton University in 1930 as his 'Manual of the Organic House', six were set forth by Baillie Scott in 'The Studio' thirty years earlier:

1. To reduce … the separate rooms to a minimum and make all come together as enclosed space.

2. To associate the building as a whole with its site.

3. To eliminate the room as a box and the house as another.

6. To eliminate combinations of different materials in favor (sic) of mono-material … to use no ornament that did not come out of the nature of materials.

7 — Kornwolf, **M. H. Baillie Scott and the Arts and Crafts Movement**, p.393.

8 — IBID, p.195.

9 — IBID, p.195, 196.

10 — IBID, P.389.

11 — Creece, **The Search for Environment**, p.297. This includes a quote from M. H. Baillie Scott, 'The Decoration of the Suburban House', **The Studio**, 5 (April 1895), pp. 15-22 (p.20).

12 — Peter Gössel and Gabriele Leuthäuser, **Architecture in the Twentieth Century**, (Cologne: Benedikt Taschen, 1991), p.68.

13 — IBID, p.425.

14 — Kornwolf, **M. H. Baillie Scott and the Arts and Crafts Movement**, p.392.

15 — IBID.

16 — IBID, p.393.

17 — IBID, p.316.

8. To incorporate as organic architecture … furnishings, making them all one with the building and designing them in simple terms for machine work.

9. Eliminate the decorator. He was all curves and all efflorescence, if not all period."[7]

The question of whether Baillie Scott's plans were more advanced than Wright's remains "unanswerable,"[8] but, Kornwolf considered Baillie Scott to be "slightly in advance of Wright in his renunciation of period detail and of heavy monumentality."[9] It is also known that "Baillie Scott's works were illustrated in books owned by Wright, … at a time when Wright's library was very small."[10] "Nor is it perhaps politic to mention that in 1895, … [Baillie Scott] was advocating the insertion of small, heraldic or floral designs of rich colouring, in squares or diamonds of clear glass, in casement windows, so as to 'have a brilliant jewel-like effect', and that Frank Lloyd Wright later called his coloured insets of glass in leaded panes his 'jewels'."[11] "Wright's early houses were named after the flat prairies of the American midwest."[12] These he first "described fully in the article 'A home in a Prairie Town' in the [American] magazine 'Ladies' Home Journal' in 1900"[13] Kornwolf made a comparison of a "fully developed, typical 'Prairie School' house,"[14] designed by Wright for W. H. Hardy in Racine, Wisconsin (1905), with Baillie Scott's design for 'Myrtle Bank' and 'Holly Bank', prepared 10 years previously: "here are the same roughcast surfaces relieved by half-timber-work, the same low gable roof, the same kind of judicious planning with living areas placed towards the garden rather than towards the road, the same effort to integrate house and site, the same response to materials and their textures, the same reliance upon pure proportion and simplicity of massing, the same contrast of low and high ceilings and the planning by area and level rather than by room and floor."[15] Wright unquestionably advanced the principles initiated by the Arts and Crafts movement but "whether it was the Arts and Crafts or the 'Prairie School' which took the fundamental step for later architecture remains controversial."[16]

Nikolaus Pevsner elevated Voysey, Baillie Scott, Mackintosh and others, via their role in the 'Morris' or Arts and Crafts movement, "to the status of pioneers of the Modern

18 — Kornwolf, **M. H. Baillie Scott and the Arts and Crafts Movement**, p.317.

19 — Kornwolf, 'M. H. Baillie Scott', p.130.

20 — Kornwolf, **M. H. Baillie Scott and the Arts and Crafts Movement**, p.189.

21 — IBID.

22 — IBID, p.193.

23 — Taken from Kornwolf., 'M. H. Baillie Scott', p.130, but the original source is, unfortunately, unidentified.

Movement."[17] Betjeman believed Baillie Scott "would not himself appreciate such a distinction,"[18] "yet early Modernist work affirms Arts and Crafts influence in planning by area and level rather than by room and floor, in retaining simple, white, unadorned walls with flush set windows, [and] in advocating 'total design',"[19] all pioneered in the works of Baillie Scott. At the 'White Lodge', Wantage, Berkshire (1898–1899), for instance, "the exterior is exclusively roughcast, without a hint of period detail or ornamentation"[20] and like the White House, Helensburgh, already described, achieved a pureness of form that gave "the mass its characteristic cubic and geometric regularity."[21] Inside, the rooms were "transformed into spaces, the walls into masses (and) the floors into levels"[22] which, combined with his self-designed decoration and built-in furniture, serves to illustrate how Baillie Scott might deserve the title bestowed upon him and his contemporaries by Pevsner. It was not without good reason that Le Corbusier described Baillie Scott in 1912 as one of "les plus grands artists"[23] and as such, deserves some of the credit that the more dynamic figures of this period command.

15/8/98

Design — Jonathon Jeffrey
© Amulree Publications
First published 1995

£5.95

ISBN 0-9521126-5-5

Although born in Kent and trained in Bath, Baillie Scott's architectural development spiralled whilst living, for 12 years, in the Isle of Man. His work was much published and built throughout The British Isles, Europe and further afield and included competition winning schemes and important Royal commissions.

This publication is part of a growing movement whose aim is to celebrate the pioneering spirit of this innovative, yet critically underaclaimed, Arts and Crafts architect and sheds new light on his career, through the illustration of previously unpublished schemes.